HOW TO LIVE AS AN EMOTIONAL MILLIONAIRE

Uncover the Hidden Riches Behind Resolving Resentments in Relationships

ALICE WIAFE

ISBN-13: 978-0990361909
ISBN-10: 099036190X

TABLE OF CONTENTS

CHAPTER 1   THE FINANCIAL SYSTEM

CHAPTER 2   BUYER BEWARE!

CHAPTER 3   DEBT MANAGEMENT

CHAPTER 4   DEBT FORGIVENESS

CHAPTER 5   SET UP A LOVE ACCOUNT

CHAPTER 6   SPIRITUAL REFERENCES

Thank You and Words of Appreciation

I want to thank everyone that I have had the privilege and honor of loving and being loved by throughout my life. I haven't always been wise with my words or behavior, and I thank those who have been patient with me throughout my journey.

HOW TO USE THIS BOOK

Thank you for purchasing this self-help book. It is an honor for me to share with you what I have learned about the topic of anger and other painful emotions in the context of relational discord. For the last ten years, I have been a consultant of Anger Management, and I have had the privilege of supporting hundreds of men and women through their emotional healing journey. I am not only a teacher of how to overcome anger and un-forgiveness, but I have also had to walk that same road. I encourage you to read and apply the suggestions in this book.

It will contribute to you:

- **Feeling** wealthier in relationships
- **Being** wiser in emotional investments
- **Experiencing** a richer overall quality of life

This book was written to be used independently or as part of our coaching program. It is designed to be simple and easy to read. However, it is important to pace yourself so you can get the most out of your reading and subsequent application. If you decide to venture on this journey independently, you will have the option of completing this mission in six-month increments, e.g. six months, twelve months, eighteen months, etc. Our suggestion is that you read through the entire book initially to get an overall understanding of the mission, then cautiously proceed through the chapters once again with an accountability partner, someone who has vowed to take the journey with you to keep you on track. If you decide to take the challenge through our coaching program, you will have the opportunity to work with likeminded participants taking the same journey as well as your own certified coach. Our online learning portal offers many opportunities to learn though video, chat, webinars, quizzes, and much more. To inquire or register for our coaching program you can visit our site info@angermanagement.ca.

I honor you for your courage to take this leap of faith.

Alice Wiafe

PROLOGUE:
THE CURRENCY OF ANGER

The lack of understanding about anger keeps many of us victims. Most of us feel powerless against this emotion, and this feeling of powerlessness causes us even more frustration. For this reason, it is important we understand anger and its purpose.

Anger is an emotion defined as "a strong feeling of annoyance, displeasure or hostility." Anger exists on a continuum which ranges from mild irritation to rage. Just like we have physical pain which tells us that something is wrong with our physical health, anger is an emotional pain that tells us something is wrong with our emotional health. A feeling of anger suggests we are in a dangerous emotional zone and that it's not safe or healthy to feel that way.

Currency refers to "the medium of exchange that is acceptable in a financial system." For instance, if a candy costs one dollar, a dollar bill can be offered as fair value for the exchange of the candy. This is an acceptable exchange for both parties. In the same way, when someone causes us emotional pain, our anger is the only acceptable currency. When exchanged tactfully, an opportunity is presented to resolve the issue or part ways.

Anger is an internal sign that an emotional threat has presented itself. We are hardwired with sensitivity to painful stimuli referred to as our "fight-or-flight response." When our fight-or-flight mechanism detects a threat, it signals our anger to assume responsibility for executing methods to protect us by fighting or fleeing from the threat. It might look something like this:

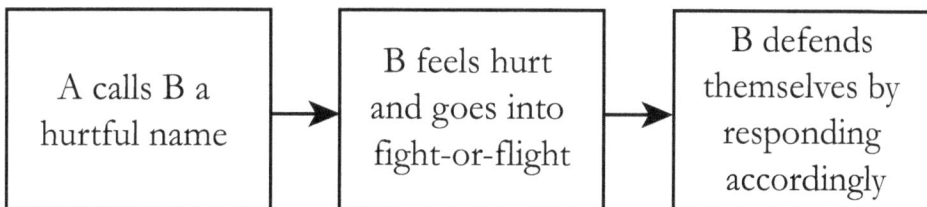

A calls B a hurtful name	→	B feels hurt and goes into fight-or-flight	→	B defends themselves by responding accordingly

For this reason, anger acts as a protective shield, and it is in our best interest to be able to feel anger so we can act. However, many people negate or deny anger because they associate it only with negative behaviors. As a result of this misconception, anger is prevented from accomplishing its true goal which is to alert and protect us from potential harm and oppositional threats.

Difficulty in relationships is a reality many of us will have to face. Whether that relationship is with a spouse, parent, child or close friend, emotional opposition presented by such individuals can have a dramatic impact on our emotional wellbeing. Learning to solve problems effectively in difficult relationships must be done skillfully—not impulsively. The goal of this book is to provide practical tools to help people heal from broken relationships and thrive emotionally.

THE EMOTIONAL MILLIONAIRE MISSION

What Is an Emotional Millionaire?

An Emotional Millionaire is a person who is committed to liberating themself from emotional pain by working out painful or difficult relationships.

Why Become an Emotional Millionaire?

There are many reasons why we should pursue emotional calm. Some of these reasons include, but are not limited to, the following:

- It allows us to enjoy the relationships that are healthy
- It allows us to find passion and clarity in the work we do.
- It makes us aware of our own emotional shortcoming so we don't harm ourselves or others.
- It teaches us how to successfully resolve emotional problems amicably and with minimal collateral damage.

THE MISSION: You have just inherited $10,000 worth of anger in a checking account. For the purposes of this book, I am an emotional investment counselor. I am personally sending you on a mission, where only if it is completed will you then have access to your millions and be officially declared "An Emotional Millionaire."

THE CHALLENGE: Perform an emotional inventory of all the relationships in your life, past and present. Identify those relationships that have pain attached to them. Within the next six months, you are going to attempt to resolve every relational discord in your life by using the techniques in this book.

PROVISION: Your Emotions, Anger Management Tools, Forgiveness, Ingredients of Love

POTENTIAL ROADBLOCKS: Prideful Judgments of Self-Righteousness, Fear of Rejection, Fear of Reconciliation, Circumstances Beyond Your Control, Fear of the Truth, Fear of Vulnerability, Rebelliousness, Denial

SUCCESS: A successful completion of this mission would mean that you:

- Successfully identified all relationships that had painful emotional ties.
- Used the tools in this book to resolve every broken relationship within your power.
- Now stand confidently and truthfully knowing you have nothing against anyone in your heart.
- Have made attempts to approach and resolve with those who had something against you except for cases where safety may be of concern.
- Continue and endeavor to practice living a life free of offence.

RESULT - **Mentally** at peace, **Emotionally** joyful and thankful, **Behaviorally** self-Controlled, **Spiritually** living in Love

Additional Details: Your $10,000 worth of anger acts as money. Treat your anger like actual cash on a vacation getaway. If you spend it before your time is up, you will be stranded. Stranded would mean that you have overspent your anger, and other parties will naturally retaliate, creating a vicious cycle of tit for tat. Anger always requires you to act, so it will always cost you something. However, positive spending of anger will cost you little (e.g. time, patience) while negative spending of anger costs much more (e.g. relationships, job, health). Be careful to use your anger only when necessary and beware of your spending habits. If you use your anger sensibly, upon arrival at the end of Chapter 4, you will owe no one.

Special Instructions:

- Calculate how much anger you will spend on a daily, weekly, and monthly basis in order to stay on track for the challenge.
- If you decide to take more than six months to complete the mission, you may write a check with the corresponding ratio, e.g. six months= $10,000, twelve months =$20,000

- Chapters 1 and 2 highlight everything you need to know about your emotions. Chapters 3 and 4 introduce the tools you can use to manage and resolve all your emotional conflicts. Chapter 5 introduces you to a new way of living in order to truly experience being an Emotional Millionaire. Chapter 6 highlights spiritual references that support the recommendations in this book.

Fill in the check below confirming you have received payment in full and are ready to proceed on your journey.

Bank of Life Inc
Survive Me Avenue

Date _____ 7

PAY TO THE
ORDER OF _____ $ _____ ,000

_____ *thousand* _____ DOLLARS

SIGNED *Emotional Millionaire Series* _____

ANGER PRICE LIST

This chart lists all the various ways we can spend anger. If you plan to meet the time specifications for completing this workbook in 6 months, $10,000 worth of anger amounts to an overall expenditure of $1666/month, $416/week, or $60/day. Negative and positive spending habits are presented below.

Instructions on using this Price List: *Most of us engage in the same angry behaviors most of the time. Highlight the ones you find yourself using on occasions when you are triggered. At the end of each day, reflect on your actions and reactions with the individuals you came across and fill in the required information on the sheet called* **"Account Statement"** *at the back of each chapter. You may want to make extra copies. Insert the anger items you used that day and maintain a running list until the end of the month, then make a total calculation.*

Negative Anger Items	Cost $	Description
Accusing	50	To claim someone has done something wrong
Advice Giving	15	To give an opinion about what could or should be done about a problem
Assuming	50	To accept information as true without verification or proof
Arrogance	25	To display a sense of overbearing self-worth or self-importance
Arguing	25	To engage in a quarrel or verbal dispute
All or nothing	25	To see things in only black and white, your way or no way
Avoiding	50	To intentionally stay away from people or circumstances
Blaming	50	To find someone at fault or responsible
Breaking things	75	To violently smash or destroy something
Back Biting	50	To engage in malicious talk about someone who is not present
Biting	100	To wound or pierce with your teeth
Bringing up past	50	To keep dragging old stories or experiences back up

Negative Anger Items	Cost $	Description
Comparing	25	To examine similarities and differences between two parties
Crying	50	To wail or sob in pain
Cutting	100	To pierce or sever with an instrument causing someone injury
Cutting your Eye	25	To give a look of disgust and disappointment or disapproval
Criticizing	50	To judge with disapproval or to find fault with
Complaining	25	To grumble and express dissatisfaction
Cold Shoulder	50	To brush off, disregard, ignore, shun, turn up one's nose
Choking	100	To restrict or obstruct someone's breathing
Controlling people	75	To enforce your will on another person
Controlling situations	75	To forcefully manipulate and regulate circumstances
Denial	50	To refuse or accept the truth about a situation or person
Demanding	50	To ask for with urgency or authority
Dismissing	50	To refuse to accept or recognize someone's point of view
Eyeing up and down	25	To look at someone up and down with disgust
Fantasizing evil	50	To wish or imagine negative things happening to someone
Forcing Physically	100	To exert your power against someone so they will comply
Folding Arms	25	To engage in body language with your arms which signifies disapproval
Frowning	25	To wrinkle the brow to express displeasure
Fisting Hand	75	To make a threatening gesture with your fist
Forgetfulness	50	To act neglectful or fail to remember
Generalizing	25	To make broad conclusions or statements about things

Negative Anger Items	Cost $	Description
Get in someone's face	75	To approach someone in very close proximity with intent of intimidation
Gang up on	75	To join in a group to overpower someone else
Gossiping	50	To maliciously spread rumors of a personal nature about someone
Glaring Eyes	25	To stare fixedly and angrily
Groaning	25	To express a deep sound of pain, displeasure or being weighed down
Guarded	50	To act cautious and distrustful of others
Grabbing Someone	100	To take, snatch or grasp or obtain by force
Hand in Face	50	To utilize an aggressive gesture conveying disrespect
Humiliating	50	To lower someone's pride, dignity or self-respect
Hand on hip	25	To utilize a gesture on the body to convey annoyance
Hitting someone	100	To physically strike someone
Hitting something	75	To strike an object with aggression
Intimidating	75	To cause someone to be filled with fear
Ignoring	50	To refuse to pay attention to or disregard
Ingratitude	25	To express a lack of thankfulness
Internalizing	25	To hold on to an unresolved issue rather than releasing it
Impatience	25	To show intolerance or irritability with people
Judging	50	To label people as good or bad and to treat them accordingly
Jumping to conclusions	50	To come to a conclusion about something without checking out the facts
Know-it-All	15	To think you know everything all the time
Kicking things	75	To assault by striking with your feet

Negative Anger Items	Cost $	Description
Kissing your teeth	25	To make a sound with your mouth to show anger or disapproval
Looking away	25	To redirect your face as to express disinterest or annoyance
Labeling	50	To categorize someone in an absolutely negative manner
Magnifying	25	To make a problem worse by blowing it out of proportion
Minimizing	25	To underestimate the magnitude of a problem
Middle Finger	75	To display an obscene hand gesture equivalent to a swear word
Mocking	25	To taunt or express ridicule
Mumbling	25	To speak words underneath your breath to convey anger or annoyance
Mindreading	25	To assume we know why a person is behaving or acting in a manner
Making Excuses	50	To put off or find reasons not to do or to keep doing something
Moving Slowly	50	To act passively by taking a longer time to do something
Name Calling	50	To use abusive names to belittle or degrade another person
Pacing	15	To walk back and forth as an expression of annoyance or anxiety
Profanity	75	To use blasphemous or obscene language.
Pranking	15	To play a mischievous trick or a joke on someone
Putting Down	50	To criticize or belittle someone
Pointing the finger	50	To blame someone for something
Punching a wall	75	To violent strike a wall out of anger or rage
Pretense of any kind	25	To deliberately mislead or deceive people

Negative Anger Items	Cost $	Description
Physically Attacking	100	To launch an attack on someone's physical body
Projecting	50	To redirect anger you have for one person onto another
Plotting Revenge	100	To plan to punish someone for the wrong done unto you
Pushing	100	To exert force on another person in order to move them
Procrastinating	75	To put off or delay an action to a later time
Rolling Eyes	25	To show a nonverbal gesture used to communicate anger or annoyance
Refusing Eye contact	25	To refuse to look into someone's eye
Raising Voice	50	To talk louder, either to be heard more clearly or in anger
Road Rage	100	To act aggressively toward motorists or pedestrians while driving
Ruminating	75	To go over and over something in your mind.
Rebelling	100	To refuse, oppose, and act in disobedience to others' wishes
Resenting	100	To feel continual anger and bitterness towards someone
Slapping	100	To execute a sharp blow with an open hand towards someone
Sarcasm	50	To communicate a cutting, often ironic remark intended to wound.
Sexual Abuse	100	To force unwanted sexual activity on another
Sulking	25	To remain in a mood of withdrawal or silence
Sighing	25	To exhale a long, deep breath conveying weariness
Swearing	75	To use abusive, violent, or blasphemous language against someone
Shaking Fist	75	To gesture with the hand to provoke an altercation
Saying whatever	25	To use this comment is to convey indifference or a lack of care

Negative Anger Items	Cost $	Description
Stonewalling	50	To refuse to answer questions or to give evasive replies
Shaking Head	25	To gesture with the head to convey disappointment or disapproval
Spitting in face	100	To eject saliva as a sign of anger, hatred, disrespect or contempt
Slamming Doors	75	To forcibly and loudly shut a door
Self-abuse	100	To inflict harm or damage on one's self
Stabbing	100	To thrust a knife or other weapon at a person to wound
Silence	50	To refuse to communicate by talking, a type of punishment
Shrugging shoulders	25	To gesture with the shoulders that you don't know or you don't care
Self-Pitying	75	To pity oneself by dwelling on one's sorrows and misfortunes
Standing up	25	To assume and position yourself in such a manner to seem threatening
Shooting	100	To hit, wound or kill with a missile fired from a weapon
Trespassing	75	To enter the owner's land or property without permission.
Teasing	50	To make fun of or attempt to provoke a person
Tsk Tsk	50	To make a t-like sound to express disapproval and disappointment
Threatening gestures	75	To use gestures to seem threatening or dangerous
Threatening posture	75	To use physical positioning to seem threatening or dangerous
Threatening words	75	To use words to seem threatening or dangerous
Throwing Things	75	To hurl or fling an object with aggression or with great speed
Tapping foot/finger	15	To use your foot or finger to gesture or convey annoyance at waiting

Negative Anger Items	Cost $	Description
Turning away	15	To redirect your head away to convey disapproval
Ultimatums	75	To demand one way or the next, with the rejection resulting in a penalty
Verbal Abuse	100	To use words to cause harm to the person being spoken to.
Walking Out	50	To leave suddenly, often as an expression of disapproval
Positive Anger Items	Cost $	Description
Assertiveness	5	To lovingly and truthfully confront those who have offended you
Anger ladder	5	To use a scale to gauge anger levels and appropriate responses
Choosing your battles	5	To thoughtfully decide whether a confrontation has merit
Confession	5	To share private thoughts and behaviors with another individual
Diaphragmatic breathing	5	To use belly or deep breathing by contracting the diaphragm
Fair fighting Rules	5	To utilize rules and boundaries when engaging in conflict
Forgiveness	5	To let go of the need for revenge against someone
Needs assessment chart	5	To document people we trust to share our emotional pain with
Avoid stinking Thinking	5	To refrain from using stinking thinking patterns
Self-care	5	To utilize a regiment to maintain balance and care for the body
Self-reflection	5	To appraise or reflect on one's own actions and behaviors
Time out	5	To leave a potentially explosive scene for calm and deep reflection

Chapter 1

THE FINANCIAL SYSTEM

A financial system is one that enables lenders and borrowers to exchange funds. As borrowers, we can find ourselves anxious as we hide from ruthless collection calls and interest penalties. As lenders, we can become frustrated by people who can't or won't pay back what they owe. It's never a pleasant experience being on either end of this spectrum.

These relations in finance resemble interpersonal transgressions all too well. Quite often, the case is that when we hurt someone, a debt is created, and payback is pursued in some fashion.

This chapter will highlight how anger is used as the exchange in painful emotional encounters.

IDENTIFY YOUR PREFERRED PAYMENT OPTION

When making payments, some of us like to use check, money, debit or credit; it's a matter of preference. It is the same with anger. We all respond differently stylistically when we are triggered. Some people are quiet and timid while others are loud and overbearing. It's all anger nonetheless. Negative anger styles are grouped primarily into three categories: **Passiveness, Aggressiveness,** and **Passive-Aggressiveness.**

AGGRESSIVE TYPES

Aggressive people have a need to abuse those individuals with whom they are angry. Their behaviors include yelling screaming, hitting, pushing, throwing, and even killing. Webster's Dictionary describes *aggression* as "hostile, injurious, or destructive behavior or outlook, especially when caused by frustration." To act aggressively means that you attempt to harm the person that you believed or perceived as causing you pain. These individuals attack their victims by verbally or physically abusing them. Aggressive people tend to be impulsive and often act without thinking which gets them in a lot of trouble. As a result of their impulsive nature and destructive behaviors, people fear them and their unpredictability.

PASSIVE TYPES

Passive people have a need to ignore and deny that a problem exists when they are angry with someone. These individuals fight by not fighting and not expressing their anger outwardly. Instead,it festers internally, eventually turning on them. Passive people don't like confrontation and live with a fear of expressing their anger. They allow themselves to be taken advantage of and will often allow unhealthy behaviors by others to continue because they don't defend themselves. The long- term prognosis for passive people is depression because their behaviors send a very strong message that says "I don't care about myself."

With the passive person, it's only a matter of time before he/she explodes. By that time, everyone is confused because the person hasn't been expressing his/her discontentment. Passive people don't realize that their corrective role in a relationship is critical if others are to change.

PASSIVE-AGGRESSIVE

Passive-aggressive people have a need to control and frustrate the individuals with whom they are angry. Their behaviors include procrastinating, giving the cold shoulder, plotting, backbiting, gossiping, and moving slowly. This style is also referred to as "Backdoor Anger" because the passive- aggressive frustrates his/her victims in a sneaky fashion by controlling them psychologically.

We know we have been touched by a passive-aggressive experience because we feel like we are being punished.

ANGER SUB-STYLES

Anger styles can be further broken into sub-styles. Individuals start to fall into a pattern of predictable behaviors characterized by certain expressions, thoughts, or motivations.

Anger Avoidance

These people don't like anger much. Some are afraid of their anger or the anger of others. It can be scary, and they are afraid to lose control if they get angry. Some think it's bad to become angry. Anger avoiders gain the sense that being good or nice helps them feel safe and calm.

Anger can help us to survive when something is wrong. Avoiders can't be assertive because they feel too guilty when they say what they want. Too often the result is that they are walked over by others.

Sneaky Anger

Anger sneaks never let others know they are angry. Sometimes they don't even know how angry they are, but the anger comes out in other forms, such as forgetting things a lot or saying they'll do something but never intending to follow through. They sit around and enjoy frustrating everybody.

Anger sneaks can look hurt and innocent and often ask, "Why are you getting mad at me?" They gain a sense of control over their lives when they frustrate others. By doing little or nothing or putting things off, they thwart other people's plans. However, anger sneaks lose track of their own wants and needs. They don't know what to do with their own lives, and their lack of understanding themselves leads to boredom, frustration and unsatisfying relationships.

Paranoid Anger

This type of anger occurs when someone feels irrationally threatened by others. They seek aggression everywhere. They believe people want to take what is theirs. They expect others will attack them physically or verbally. Because of this belief, they spend much time jealously guarding and defending what they think is theirs—the love of a partner (real or imagined), their money, or their valuables.

People with paranoid anger give away their anger. They think everybody else is angry instead of acknowledging their own rage. They have found a way to get angry without guilt. Their anger is disguised as self-protection. They are insecure and trust no one. They have poor judgment because they confuse their own feelings with those of others. They see their own anger in the eyes and words of their friends, mates, and co-workers. This leaves them and everyone around them feeling confused.

Sudden Anger

People with sudden anger are like thunderstorms on a summer day. They zoom in from nowhere, blast everything in sight and then vanish. Sometimes, it's only lightning and thunder, a big show that soon blows away, but often people get hurt, homes are broken up and things are damaged that will take a long time to repair.

Sudden-anger people gain a surge of power. They release all their feelings, so they feel good or relieved. Loss of control is a major problem with sudden anger. They can be a danger to themselves and others. They may get violent. They say and do things they later regret, but by then, it's too late to take them back.

Shame-Based Anger

People who need a lot of attention or are very sensitive to criticism often develop this style of anger. The slightest criticism sets off their shame. Unfortunately, they don't like themselves very much. They feel worthless, not good enough, broken and unlovable. So when someone ignores them or says something negative, they take it as proof that the other person dislikes them as much as they dislike themselves, but that makes them really angry, so they lash out.

They think "You made me feel awful, so I'm going to hurt you back." They get rid of their shame by blaming, criticizing, and ridiculing others. Their anger helps them get revenge against anybody they think has shamed them. They avoid their own feelings of inadequacy by belittling others.

Raging against others to hide shame doesn't work very well. They usually end up attacking the people they love. They continue to be oversensitive to insults because of their poor self-image. Their anger and loss of control only makes them feel worse about themselves.

Deliberate Anger

This anger is planned. People who use this anger style usually know what they are doing. They aren't really emotional about their anger—at least not at first. They like controlling others, and the best way they've discovered to do that is with anger and sometimes violence. Power and control are what people gain from deliberate anger. Their goal is to get what they want by threatening or overpowering others.

This may work for a while, but this usually breaks down in the long run. People don't like to be bullied, and eventually they will figure out ways to escape or get back at the bully.

Addictive Anger

Some people want or need the strong feelings that come with anger. They like the intensity even if they don't like the trouble their anger causes them. Their anger is much more than a bad habit; it provides emotional excitement. It isn't fun, but it's powerful.

These people look forward to the anger "rush" and the emotional "high." Anger addicts gain a sense of intensity and emotional power when they explode. They feel alive and full of energy. Addictions are inevitably painful and damaging. This addiction is no exception. They don't learn other ways to feel good, so they become dependent upon their anger. They pick fights just to get high on anger, and since they need intensity, their anger takes on an all-or-nothing pattern that creates more problems than it solves.

Habitual Anger

Anger can become a bad habit. Habitually angry people find themselves getting angry often, usually about small things that don't bother others. They wake up grumpy, they go through the day looking for fights, they look for the worst in everything and everybody, and they usually go to bed angry about something. They might even have angry dreams. Their angry thoughts set them up for more and more arguments.

They can't seem to quit being angry, even though they are unhappy. Habitually angry people gain predictability because they always know what they feel. Life may be lousy but it is known, safe and steady. However, they get trapped in their anger, and it runs their lives. They can't get close to the people they love because their anger keeps them away.

Moral Anger

Some people think they have a right to be angry when others have broken a rule. That makes the offenders bad, evil, wicked and sinful. They have to be scolded and maybe punished. People with this anger style feel outraged about people who behave badly.

They say they have a right to defend their "beliefs," and they claim moral superiority. They gain the sense that anger is for a good cause. They don't feel guilty when they get angry because of this. They often feel superior to others even in their anger.

These people suffer from black-and-white thinking, which means they see the world too simply. They fail to understand people who are different from themselves, and they often have rigid ways of thinking and doing things. Another problem with this anger style is crusading—attacking every problem or difference of opinion with moral anger when compromise or understanding might be more effective.

(Substyles Adapted from the Anger Handbook, Effron Potter)

ALWAYS CONSIDER OVERDRAFT/INTEREST CHARGES

It can be extremely painful when a purchase of $10 ends up costing us $40 because we are hit with a $30 overdraft fee. Lenders can be merciless when a client fails to responsibly monitor his/her account balance before making purchases. Most financial institutions will take back what is owed and then penalize you harshly on top of that.

The magnitude of such a penalty can be what we are confronted with when we decide to throw the first punch at someone. We never know what we are going to get back. If and when those we offend decide to retaliate, they can do so with greater potency than we ever expected, and a vicious cycle can ensue. Let's look at a fictitious example of Fred and Theresa:

Fred got into a little tiff with his wife, Theresa, and after getting frustrated, he decided to call her an "idiot" She turned around and said, "Who are you calling an idiot?" She grabbed a pot to swing at him. As Fred tried to protect himself from the throw, he ended up pushing her. It was then that Theresa started to feel frightened and called 9-1-1. The police arrived and ended up escorting Fred to the police station. They read him his rights and told him to come back to court in two months' time. In the meanwhile, he wasn't able to go back to his house, and he wasn't able to see his kids. On top of that, he needed to find a new place to stay for the next two months, and pay for transportation because his wife used the car to pick up his kids. Now Fred is left with the responsibility of having to explain to his family and friends what happened.

This story is the perfect portrayal of how one hurtful act can snowball into an uncontrollable situation when anger is misused.

There are many reasons why we may consider managing our emotions, and they include:

- Wanting a better relationship with our family members
- Wanting to get along with peers and colleagues
- Wanting clarity in our God-given destiny in terms of the work we are to do
- Wanting to minimize job losses
- Wanting to stay out of criminal systems
- Wanting to feel physically healthier
- Wanting peace of mind
- Wanting to feel happier
- Wanting self-control

NEVER BUY ON WEAKNESS

Our unmet emotional needs stem from childhood. Early painful experiences leave memories that stay with us for life in our subconscious mind, e.g. abandonment or sexual abuse. In adulthood, these unmet emotional needs result in our making decisions based solely on meeting those needs because we are weak in those areas. For instance, we might be attracted to someone's money because we grew up impoverished, or be attracted to someone we can control because we were controlled growing up.

Performing a thorough examination of our emotional needs will reveal which parts are weak. Consequently, taking the time and energy to meet those needs will increase our overall self-worth so we are no longer vulnerable to being hurt and disappointed in relationships.

Much of our anger is triggered when others say or do things to make us feel vulnerable in one of these five areas. Our anger alerts us that the particular need is in deficit and requires a generous dose of our time and attention

We will discuss five emotional needs that may cause us to respond irrationally if not properly dealt with.

FIVE EMOTIONAL NEEDS

NEED FOR PROTECTION	*We all have a need to feel protected and shielded from harm. Relationships which are fear-based or dreadful keep us in constant panic provoking a chronically angry state. When we are able to distance ourselves from abusive or neglectful relationships, we have more peace and clarity and our anger subsides.*
NEED FOR SIGNIFICANCE	*We all have a need to feel purposeful in terms of the work we do. When we are able to utilize our gifts and talents, we feel productive and life seems meaningful. When others affirm our contributions, it strengthens us to take even greater risks and accomplish even more. Healthy relationships feed our need for significance by letting us know that we matter and what we do is meaningful and significant.*
NEED FOR RESPECT	*Respect is the experience of feeling honored or regarded. For example, respect is displayed when a person shows concern for our time and our feelings. To respect is to deliberately do and say things to convey to someone that they are worthy and have value. This sense of validation strengthens us emotionally.*
NEED FOR SELF CONTROL	*Self-mastery builds our confidence and faith in ourselves. Emotional strength is birthed when we are able to withstand the storms of life without caving in. An intentional decision not to control others is emotionally rewarding because it minimizes anxiety by placing a greater burden on us to manage our own behaviors. When external situations or relationships no longer have the power to make us lose control, it is a sign of real strength.*
NEED FOR ACCEPTANCE	*The ability to accept the good and bad in ourselves is a sign of emotional health. Understanding that all human beings are flawed and have weaknesses alleviates opportunities for others to take advantage of our insecurities and make us feel bad about ourselves. The goal of life is not to be perfect, rather it is to continually improve and to become the best person we can be.*

SANDY'S STORY

Sandy grew up with her biological father and stepmother. Sandy rarely saw her biological mother who had opted for the "exciting single life" instead. Her father, who had custody of her, remarried her stepmother and had three more children.

Sandy never really felt like she belonged. Her stepmother would blatantly play favoritism with her own biological children. Sandy had memories of food being shared and getting leftovers. Though she wasn't mistreated by her father, she never wanted to cause problems between him and his wife, so she rarely spoke to him about how she felt. For the longest time, she kept the hostile treatment by her stepmother to herself and never discussed it with her father.

By age sixteen, Sandy had become a shy introvert, often intimidating people with her facial expressions to thwart off prospective inquirers. Her hostile demeanor kept people away so she could control who came in and out of her life.

Sandy found love early and grew attached to her high school sweetheart, whom she later married and with whom she had three children.

In her relationships, Sandy was very passive, caring for everyone but herself. Her husband had a thriving social life, and Sandy would feel extremely rejected when he wanted to spend time with his friends and family. Her children took advantage of her, and she would drop everything any time anyone had a need.

By her mid-thirties, Sandy started to experience burnout. It seemed everyone's needs mattered more than hers. She started to resent being taken advantage of by her husband and children and even her colleagues at work.

In a counseling session with Sandy, she uncovered that she had internalized beliefs from her childhood abandonment and abuse that she did not matter, and that her needs were not important. Her struggles in adulthood were the manifestation of this dysfunctional thought process.

When Sandy was able to connect the dots between her thought process and her current behavior, she set out to resolve her issues with her mother, her father, and her stepmother.

Suggested Activities

1. Your Anger Covenant
2. Strategy for difficult days
3. Same O' Same O'

ACCOUNT STATEMENT

MONTH_____

Anger Item	Date	Cost
E.g., Raised my voice	March 13	50
1.		
2.		
3.		
4.		
5.		
6.		
7.		
8.		
9.		
10.		
11.		

12.		
13.		
14.		
15.		
16.		
17.		
18.		
19.		
20.		
21.		
22.		
23.		
24.		
25.		
26.		
27.		
28.		

Total: _____

MY ANGER COVENANT

Making promises to ourselves is like tying down your decisions in a windstorm. Yes, you need to make a decision to manage your anger; however, making a promise to yourself in front of others secures it to a far greater degree. Some of the most important things in life are both "said" in public and "written" in a document—whether it is oaths in courts or vows in marriage. When we say things to someone else and sign our signature, we solidify our commitment. This in itself helps us accomplish our goals.

Sign the following commitment and have it witnessed by at least one other person.

I, _____, have struggled with anger and negative emotions for quite sometime now, and I am tired of it controlling my life. Today, I stop making excuses for my behavior. Today, I am going to stop blaming circumstances and others for my reactions. Today, I am making a decision to start managing my angry feelings and negative emotions. As of today, I am going to learn about who I am, why I am and what I can do to become the best me possible.

As of today, I will constrain my tongue and manage my feelings. I will set my focus on never letting my emotions get the best of me. Instead, I will use the best of me to manage it. I will not just say I am going to do it; I will do it. I will do this!

Name: _____ Date: _____

Witnessed by: _____ Date: _____

Witnessed by: _____ Date: _____

MY STRATEGY FOR DIFFICULT DAYS

If and when I am having a bad day, this will be my plan: I will nurture myself rather than beating Myself up by

(Sort in the order of your interest)

My first choice will be to   _____

My second choice will be to   _____

My third choice will be to   _____

If none of the above is an option during that time,

I may opt to   _____

                                       _____

I definitely will not   _____

                                       _____

_____

_____

SUGGESTED RECOMMEDATIONS

Read a book   Take a walk   Take a hot bath

Play a sport   Go to church   Take a break from difficult activities

Call a friend   Journal   Pray and meditate

SAME O' SAME O'

Recall the last three times you felt very angry:

Scenario #1

Who was it with?   _____

When was it?   _____

How did it start?   _____

_____

_____

While it was happening, what were you:

Thinking?   _____

Feeling?   _____

Doing?   _____

Saying?   _____

How did it end?   _____

_____

_____

Scenario #2

Who was it with?   _____

When was it?   _____

How did it start?   _____

_____

_____

While it was happening, what were you:

Thinking?   _____

Feeling?   _____

Doing?   _____

Saying?   _____

How did it end?   _____

_____

_____

Scenario #3

Who was it with?   _____

When was it?   _____

How did it start?   _____

_____

_____

While it was happening, what were you:

Thinking?   _____

Feeling?   _____

Doing?   _____

Saying?   _____

How did it end?   _____

_____

_____

Chapter 2

BUYER BEWARE!

Caveat Emptor, "Let the buyer beware," is a financial principal that notifies a buyer that the goods he or she is buying are "as is" and subject to all defects. When a sale is subject to this warning, the buyer assumes the risk that the product might be either defective or unsuitable for his or her need.

When our anger begins to escalate, it can be experienced by others as defective or out of control. This is the reason we need to consistently monitor our anger. This chapter will focus on the four areas that provide feedback on the status of our anger: We must always beware of our Anger malfunctioning in these four areas; Physical, Behavioral, Emotional, and Mental/Cognitive.

BEWARE OF PHYSICAL MALFUNCTIONING

Many physical signs tell us that our anger is escalating or getting out of control. When our fight-or- flight response is triggered, there is a decrease of blood flow into our brain and an increase of blood flow into the muscles of our bodies including our arms, legs and heart. This transition prepares us to run or fight when confronted with a threat. While we have the ability to fight harder and move quicker, we lose the ability to think rationally and logically. It is very important that we monitor these physical changes because they tell us how far we are straying from an emotionally safe zone. These bodily changes initiate a stress state which tempts us into wanting to attack rather than problem-solve. Thus, early detection of these physical symptoms can empower us to make better choices before the situation gets out of hand.

Some of the bodily changes are listed below:

Physical Cues	Rapid Heart Rate
	Sweating
	Dilated Pupils
	Clenching of Jaws and Teeth
	Flushed Face
	Headache
	Stomachache
	Dizziness
	Tension
	Rolling Eyes
	Raised Eyebrows
	Facial Gestures
	Shaking and Trembling

In addition to bodily changes, there are also certain physical conditions such as hunger, anxiety, loneliness and fatigue which predispose us to respond in an angry manner. To make it easier to remember these four states, an acronym has been created called **HALT** (**H** for **h**ungry, **A** for **a**nxious, **L** for **l**onely and **T** for **t**ired). If we find ourselves in any of these conditions, it is recommended that we halt and meet those needs first before attempting to solve a problem.

Hungry Anxious Lonely Tired

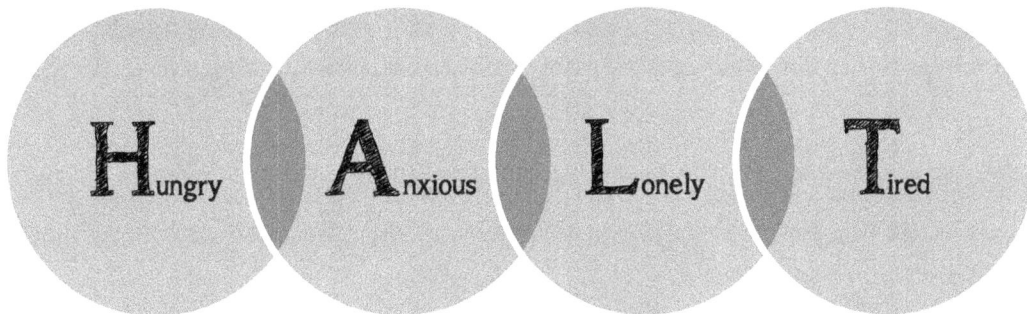

BEWARE OF BEHAVIORAL MALFUNCTIONING

We act out in various ways as our anger escalates. This includes the behaviors in the list below:

Behavioral Warning Signs			
	Hitting	Slamming doors	Looking away
	Screaming	Driving dangerously	Belittling
	Swearing	Bodily cutting	Ignoring
	Sarcasm	Cleaning	Projecting
	Drinking	Pacing back and forth	Crying
	Drugging	Punching walls	Finger pointing
	Sleeping		
	Eating		
		Breaking things	Throwing things
		Listening to violent music	
	Plotting	Watching Violent Movies	
	Complaining	Joking	
	Withdrawing	Blaming	
	Silence	Threatening	

In a general sense, the things we do when we are angry are learned behaviors. They are habitual patterns of responding as a result of lacking effective problem-solving skills. What we do during an anger episode is most likely what we saw a parent or significant adult figure do at one time in our lives and so end up repeating.

As we try to change our anger habits, it is helpful to picture anger like a dance between two people. If one person changes a step, it confuses the other party and forces them to do something different as well.

If our anger behaviors have been learned, they can also be unlearned. This will require a conscious monitoring of how we currently engage with others while we are angry. Once we are able to see ourselves objectively, we can assess which behaviors are constructive or destructive and take steps to implement changes.

BEWARE OF EMOTIONAL MALFUNCTIONING

Our emotions play a critical role in the anger experience. When we are emotionally healthy, we feel happy and self controlled. However, when we have emotional wounds, people can do or say things to trigger a host of painful emotions within us and cause us to lose control. A sample of emotions is listed below:

PRIMARY **Emotions**			
	Abandoned	Dread	Judged
	Assaulted	Exhausted	Loss of Control
	Abused	Empty	Lonely
	Afraid	Embarrassed	Neglected
	Alone	Fearful	Manipulated
	Annoyed	Fatigued	Oppressed
	Angry	Guilt	Pressured
	Anxious	Grief	Rejected
	Ashamed	Hopeless	Sad
	Betrayed	Helpless	Trapped
	Belittled	Humiliated	Used
	Cheated	Heartbroken	Useless

Controlled	Hurt	Violated
Confused	Incompetent	Vulnerable
Deceived	Inadequate	Ugly
Deprived	Insecure	Unaccepted
Disappointed	Intimidated	Unprotected
Disgusted	Irritated	Unappreciated
Defeated	Impatient	Worthless
Discouraged	Insignificant	Weary
Disrespected	Inferior	Weak

When we have emotional wounds from childhood, we are supersensitive when others touch that sore spot. These painful feelings become part of our emotional database to be feared as dangerous in subsequent relationships.

These raw and painful emotions are referred to as primary emotions because they are the initial feelings that caused us great pain, e.g. disrespect, incompetence, or sadness. Anger, on the other hand, is called a secondary emotion because it emerges as a protective emotion to keep us from feeling the primary emotion.

We can choose to not feel primary emotions by masking them with anger. When we do so, by default we choose not to experience other healthy emotions that assist us to love and have intimate and healthy relationships with others. We literally choke our ability to feel and become cold and insensitive. This creates emotional problems and sets the perfect stage for addictions to compensate for good feelings. Anger was meant to be a survival instinct used for problem-solving in temporary situations. Instead, many of us have embraced it as a way of life. To live in survival mode keeps us just surviving and barely living. To really start living, we have to start feeling.

Masking our feelings with anger:

- Alienates those we care about because it minimizes opportunities for closeness and Intimacy.

- Causes us to neglect offensive behavior by others because we don't feel offended when we Should.
- Makes us insensitive to other people's pain because we can't empathize with them.
- Redirects all our care and love toward inanimate objects which don't fulfill us, e.g. money, cars, houses, drugs, alcohol, food.

Thus, learning to identify and express the primary feeling beneath our anger is critical if we want to solve the root of our relational problems.

BEWARE OF COGNITIVE/MENTAL MALFUNCTIONING

Cognition refers to the thinking patterns that fuel our anger. Of the four areas addressed, our cognitions, or thoughts, have the most bearing on our emotional welfare because our emotions are derived directly from our thoughts. All systems, including behavior and character, flow from a healthy mind.

According to studies, a person thinks an average of 2,500 to 3,500 thoughts on a daily basis. Thus, a person who has decided to become conscious of their thoughts can have great success in also managing their emotions.

Learning to monitor our thoughts is the most critical step in this emotional journey. Our goal is to guard our minds against beliefs and mental habits that sabotage us. In particular, there are three areas we want to address: ATTITUDE, GRATITUDE, and FORTITUDE.

I am reminded of a popular saying which reads:

"Watch your thoughts; they become your words. Watch your words; they become your actions. Watch your actions; they become your habits. Watch your habits; they become your character. Watch your character; it becomes your destiny."

Anonymous

ATTITUDE CHECK

A poor-me attitude is a mindset of pity, and it derives its motivations from a place of inferiority. An individual who pities his/her self preys on people feeling sorry for him/her. These individuals are always victims and seem to think they are powerless and worse off than everybody else.

A not-me attitude is a mindset of pride, and it derives its motivations from a place of superiority. Prideful people think they are superior in their qualities and fail to recognize their limitations. They seem to think they are too powerful and better off than everybody else.

It's in Me and You attitude is neither pitiful nor prideful but **faithful**. Faith believes in me, and it believes in you. It understands that life casts its shadow on everyone and that there are seasons and times for everything. To be faithful means we stay true to ourselves no matter if we are up or down and keep believing that eventually all things work out to our benefit. We believe the same for others. This is a healthy attitude to have towards people.

Prideful Beliefs	Pitiful Beliefs	Faithful Beliefs
Not-Me Attitude	Poor-Me Attitude	It's in me and you Attitude
"I can do it all."	"I can't do it at all."	"We can both do it."
There's no way this can't work	This is hopeless	If someone has overcome it, I can too
Things have to work out for me	Things never work out for me	I am going to give this my best shot because it's been possible for others.

GRATITUDE CHECK

Gratitude is defined as the quality of being thankful and a readiness to show appreciation for and to return kindness.

The reason why gratitude is important is because without it, we fail to see any good in our lives and our perception of people and life becomes negative. Gratitude keeps us appreciating even the small things and challenges us to recognize how blessed we are in spite of life's difficulties.

We show gratitude when we engage in the following behaviors:

Acts of Gratitude	
	When we count our blessings and not our worries.
	When we don't buy things we don't need.
	When we consciously voice our gratitude to everyone who assists us in anyway.
	When we don't complain and grumble.
	When we give to good causes.
	When we look for the lesson in every trial.
	When we do thoughtful things for people like opening doors or assisting them with their needs.

We take for granted what many people in the world simply do not have such as food, clothing, shelter, or access to healthcare. When was the last time we had to sell our children because we did not have the money to survive or even provide for them? Chances are we have never experienced these things. Unfortunately, many people face these grim realities around the world each day. It is a great habit to thank God each day for all the terrible things that we don't have to endure!

FORTITUDE CHECK

Fortitude is the strength of mind that allows one to endure pain or adversity with courage over the long haul.

It's ultimately not giving up, and doing what we need to do to get where we want to go. It is making up our minds to keep going no matter how we feel. Many of us may know what it's like to start a new habit, quit an old one, or to press on even when it seems hopeless. The mind is one of the strongest attributes of the human experience, and a single decision not to give up proves very fruitful. After all, it's always darkest before dawn. We truly are very resilient, but we will never know this about ourselves unless we endure through difficulties.

To maximize your fortitude:

Keys to Fortitude

Make up your mind to do the emotional work life has given you. We won't get anything done unless we make a conscious decision to do so. Real success doesn't happen by accident. We have to set our minds to consciously pursue success.

Discipline yourself. Discipline is training ourselves in order to produce a specific character or pattern of behavior, particularly moral or mental improvement. It never feels good while we are in the process; however, the results that follow can be achieved no other way. The long term gain is always worth our short term pain.

Remain committed. Even if our commitment is only to do a little, be committed to the little. Don't set too high a standard, but set a standard. Failing to set a standard denies us the opportunity to truthfully assess our growth.

Ask for help. We are not an island, so we must to seek help when needed. The emotional work is difficult but very doable. We can tell someone else what we are doing and communicate to them if we are struggling. We can even seek a professional, if we need to. Asking requires great strength, and only strong people can ask for help when they need it.

MARK'S STORY

Mark grew up in a home filled with abuse. Most of his memories include being hit, yelled at, and told he would amount to nothing by his father. Mark always felt that he could never please his father. Through his adolescence, he would put forth good effort into school and work, but he could never complete anything. Even when he came into an opportunity, it wouldn't be long until something happened to sabotage his efforts. Mark resented how his father treated him. His mother would often stay quiet during his father's ranting, but Mark secretly yearned for her to protect him.

In relationships, Mark would often be attracted to passive women he could control. When they would resist his controlling ways, he would react with anger and abuse them verbally and sometimes physically.

Mark failed to keep a job for any length of time and would depend on his partners for financial support. After two failed long-term relationships, Mark had two children he was unable to support financially. He rarely saw them, and when he did, he would show up empty-handed. Both mothers had a fear of Mark's abusive nature, so they would not say anything to him when he acted in this manner.

Mark would find himself getting into bad business deals where he would always be the one to lose out. He could not understand why everything in his life always seemed to go wrong.

In counseling, Mark realized that the early treatment by his father made him internalize the belief that he was worthless. His relationships in his adult years were a manifestation of this dysfunctional belief system. When Mark was able to explore his deeper emotions of worthlessness and incompetence, he was able to approach his father to initiate a discussion about how he felt growing up.

Suggested Activities

1. Diagnosing my anger
2. Recognizing my anger style

3. How I trigger others
4. My early warning signs
5. Halt
6. Attitude check

ACCOUNT STATEMENT

MONTH_____

Anger Item	Date	Cost
E.g., Raised my voice	March 13	50
1.		
2.		
3.		
4.		
5.		
6.		
7.		
8.		
9.		
10.		
11.		
12.		

13.		
14.		
15.		
16.		
17.		
18.		
19.		
20.		
21.		
22.		
23.		
24.		
25.		
26.		
27.		
28.		

Total: _____

DIAGNOSING MY ANGER

How often have you felt anger on average in the time frame below?	Never	Once a week	Twice a week	Several times a week	Daily	Always
Last month						
Last 6 months						
Early adulthood						
Teenage years						
Childhood						

With whom do you get angry and how often?	Daily	Weekly	Monthly	Yearly	Never
My spouse/ partner					
My children					
My parents					
My siblings					
My work colleagues					
My friends					
Myself					
Strangers					
Road					
Teachers					

What did the following people do with anger when you were growing up?

Your father figure	
Your mother figure	
Your sisters	
Your brothers	
Other relatives	
People I admired	

RECOGNIZING MY ANGER STYLE

In this chapter, the text describes three different main Anger styles: Aggression, Passive-Aggression, and Passiveness. Based on the information provided in this chapter, answer the following questions.

What style are you? _____

How did you establish this conclusion? _____

What evidence supports this conclusion? _____

_____

_____

_____

_____

_____

The same text describes nine different sub-styles. Based on the information provided in this chapter, answer the following questions.

What sub-style are you? _____

How did you establish this conclusion? _____

What evidence supports this conclusion? _____

_____

_____

_____

_____

_____

Did you find yourself identifying with more than one style or sub-style? It's very common; however, we will primarily be dominant in one or two main anger styles, and various sub-styles depending on the occasion and context.

HOW I TRIGGER OTHERS

Fill in the checklist of your behaviors that make people angry.

- ☐ When I am sarcastic
- ☐ When I minimize another person's logic
- ☐ When I don't take people seriously
- ☐ When I interrupt people
- ☐ When I swear or am rude to others
- ☐ When I am late
- ☐ When I emotionally shut down and refuse to talk
- ☐ When I ignore people when they are talking
- ☐ When I am curt, sharp, cutting or critical
- ☐ When I throw things or punch a wall
- ☐ When I yell or scream
- ☐ When I don't acknowledge someone else's contribution
- ☐ When I play the devil's advocate
- ☐ When I don't praise another's worth
- ☐ When I glare at someone
- ☐ When I say nothing is wrong when there is something wrong
- ☐ When I roll my eyes
- ☐ When I show disrespect to people
- ☐ When I get preachy about my beliefs
- ☐ When I act superior to others
- ☐ When I don't do what I said I would do
- ☐ When I am insensitive to others
- ☐ When I am self-focused
- ☐ When I avoid problems
- ☐ When I procrastinate

Other things I do to make people angry:

_____

Now, think of five different people in different roles and positions in your life (significant other, sibling, co-worker, son/daughter, friend) and journal how you tend to make them angry.

Person # 1

_____

_____

_____

_____

Person # 2

_____

_____

_____

_____

Person # 3

_____

_____

_____

_____

Person # 4

_____

_____

_____

_____

Person # 5

_____

_____

_____

_____

MY EARLY WARNING SIGNS

Check the following characteristics or experiences to see if they would be an early signal for you slipping into anger. Add more of your unique early warning signs at the end of the list.

Anger:

Lack of motivation

Too little sleep

Fatigue

Self-critical

Sarcastic and judgmental

Pessimistic

Avoiding others Procrastination

Negative thoughts

Eating too much

Difficulty concentrating Unable to enjoy pleasure

Anxious or irritable

Feeling sad

Feeling hopeless

Unmotivated Crying easily

Emotionally flat Feeling insecure

Being hungry

Avoiding people

Racing heart

Tightness in chest

Difficulty concentrating

Inability to show affection

Having trouble getting out of bed

Sexually frustrated

Low energy

Suicidal thoughts

Poor appetite
Drug and alcohol abuse
A know-it-all attitude
Excessive talking   _____
Domineering   _____
Quick movements   _____
Impatience   _____

                                     _____

Itchy Fingers

We all have small everyday irritants that beg to be itched. Many of these end in angry exchanges. It could be a dirty look, someone ignoring you, or being stuck in a traffic jam. Often, much of our anger results from small irritants that build up throughout the day. Can you list the smaller irritants that TICK you off?

_____

_____

Hair Triggers

Most of us learn to navigate through some of the everyday annoyances; however, when we struggle with emotional issues, the triggers can become highly sensitive. Hair triggers are usually emotionally connected to hurts and wounds. List the people who have hurt you the most in your life. Do not be surprised if they are also the people you love the most. Then, circle one of the common wounds and draw a line to their name.

People	Common Wounds
_____	Disrespect
_____	Neglect
_____	Never good enough (perfectionism)
_____	Emotional withdrawal
_____	Critical and judgmental
_____	No approval
_____	Betrayal
_____	Broken trust
_____	Disregard
_____	Abandonment
_____	Abuse
_____	Bullying/Intimidation
_____	**WRITE YOUR OWN ON THE LINES BELOW**
_____	
_____	
_____	
_____	
_____	
_____	
_____	
_____	
_____	
_____	
_____	

H.A.L.T.

Hungry ~ Anxious ~ Lonely ~ Tired

Rate how frequently your unmet needs have contributed to your frustration and anger outbursts.

Needs	Seldom	Somewhat	Most Times
Hungry / Thirsty			
Anxious / Worried			
Lonely / Disconnected			
Tired / Fatigued			

What can you do to acknowledge and take responsibility for the fact that food affects your mood?
(How can you help yourself be nourished?)

_____

_____

_____

What can you do to get more physical and emotional rest? *(How can you help yourself be rested?)*

_____

_____

_____

What can you do when you feel lonely? *(How can you help yourself be socially connected?)*

_____

_____

_____

ATTITUDE CHECK

Document any thoughts you had this week that were prideful.

_____
_____
_____
_____
_____
_____
_____
_____
_____

Document any thoughts you had this week that were pitiful.

_____
_____
_____
_____
_____
_____
_____
_____
_____

Document any thoughts you had this week that were faithful.

_____
_____
_____
_____
_____
_____
_____
_____

Chapter 3

DEBT MANAGEMENT

D ebt Management is a unique strategy that was developed to help a debtor manage debt on an ongoing basis. When a plan is put in place, the debtor is relieved of stress and high interest rates, and the payments become manageable.

Similarly, when we are being offended by people regularly, developing a plan to manage difficult relationships and interactions can boost our sense of empowerment and help us to feel more hopeful.

This chapter will provide tools to help us manage everyday offences between family, friends, colleagues, and even strangers.

EMOTIONAL NEEDS ASSESSMENT

A needs assessment is an inquiry into our emotional weaknesses and strengths. To do this requires an examination of our daily exchanges with family, friends, co-workers, and strangers. Our goal is to discover times, situations, and events that trigger our anger. Once we discover our emotional weaknesses, we can intentionally chart out directives for meeting our needs. Becoming aware of our emotional weaknesses allows us to focus time and attention on building the kinds of relationships that will help to strengthen us.

To do this, we must first determine which of the five emotional needs require strengthening. Check the boxes that apply to a current relationship in your life. The following is a short list of sample questions to see if your current relational problems fit into any of these areas. You can add on to the various sections below.

Need for Safety

	☐ I need to be able to speak without feeling afraid
	☐ I need to feel safe from harm, intimidation and bullying
	☐ I need to be able to make mistakes without fearing consequences

Need for Respect

	☐ I need my time, feelings and possessions to be honored
	☐ I need to feel valued for more than my financial contributions.
	☐ I need my perspectives and point of view to be acknowledged and considered

Need for Significance

	☐ I need the things I do to be noticed and appreciated
	☐ I need to feel useful and purposeful
	☐ I need my feelings to matter

Need for Self-Control

	☐ I need to feel in control of my emotions and behaviors in spite of other people's conduct towards me
	☐ I need to feel self motivated to do things on my own, and without people telling me what to do
	☐ I need to stop being controlled by emotional blackmail, guilt trips, or the disapproval of others

Need for Self -Acceptance

	☐ I need to be unmoved by other people's criticisms
	☐ I need to stop feeling inferior when compared with others
	☐ I need to make choices for my life even if others disagree with me.

Emotional Assessment Chart

1. Once we are able to identify which of our emotional needs require strengthening, we can chart out our support system for meeting those needs. Those on this list will be those individuals with whom we share our emotional pain. These individuals have proven they have our best interests at heart and are safe for us to discuss our vulnerable issues with.

2. When we document our chart, it should include the unmet emotional needs, the individuals we are trusting to meet those needs, and a back-up plan in case they are unable, unavailable, or inaccessible. Our support system should include more than one person even if it means accessing agencies such as churches, counselors, etc.

3. Before we can successfully meet our emotional needs, there is one condition. We must give others what we need most, e.g., if we need to feel significant, we must make others feel significant. The more we give to others, the more we get back from others in return. For instance, we might notice someone at work and comment, "Wow, I have been noticing you've been doing a great job."

4. Make sure our support system consists of individuals who are willing and able to give and receive emotional support themselves.

We are creating our core support system. These are people we trust to meet our emotional needs. Our expectations of anyone outside this network are to be minimized.

SAMPLE SUPPORT CHART

Support Person	Relationship	Emotional Need	Back-up Plan
Donna	My sister	Need to feel safe	Let her know how I feel and journal
Mom	My mom	Need to feel accepted	Speak to Liz about it
Manchester	My son	Need to feel significant	Journal

Donna	Sister	Need to feel self-control	Speak to Mom and journal
Mom	My mom	Need to feel respected	Pray and journal

2. SELF-TALK

Self-talk is a conversation we have with ourselves about our experiences, plans, and relationships. It mimics a conversation we have with other people, except it is in our head. It happens on auto-pilot, and we are often unaware of it. Self-talk is a very powerful force in our emotions. Many angry thoughts come from hostile ideas we have about ourselves or others. Once an angry thought is planted, then angry feelings and behaviors follow.

Disputing angry self-talk, and channeling mental energy into loving thoughts toward ourselves and others can have a dramatic impact on our emotions. Instead of continuing to think these thoughts, we can dispute them, as is demonstrated in the following "Hot Thoughts/Cool Thoughts" chart.

HOT THOUGHTS	COOL THOUGHTS
I can't stand him.	*That's not fair; he is entitled to his opinion.*
Why does she always do this?	*She actually doesn't always do this. I am exaggerating.*
How dare you!	*Am I better than others? He treats everyone this way.*
That is such a stupid question.	*He genuinely may not know the answer. Sometimes I ask stupid questions.*
Why me?	*Why not me? Am I immune to pain and suffering like everyone else experiences?*

Getting into a habit of disputing with ourselves can help us gain more control over our inner bully. It also helps us to recognize the magnitude of our unhealthy thoughts towards ourselves and others.

3. STINKING THINKING

Stinking thinking involves patterns of negative thinking we develop over the years. They include, but are not limited to, the following:

OVER-GENERALIZATION	You see a single negative event as a never-ending pattern of defeat. "I'll never get a raise."
MAXIMIZING	*You exaggerate the importance of things. "Why do you always leave the fridge door open? Do you know how much money I pay for electricity?"*
MINIMIZING	*You shrink things until they appear tiny. "He only hit me four times; it's not that bad."*
JUMPING TO CONCLUSIONS	*You make a negative interpretation even though there are no definite facts that convincingly support your conclusions.* *"Mind Reader"- "I know you think I am an idiot, right?"* *"Fortune Teller"- "I know you are going to leave me!"*
SHOULDING ON PEOPLE	*You speak to others with shoulds and shouldn'ts, musts and oughts. The emotional consequence is guilt. "You should see your father; it's the right thing to do."*
MENTAL FILTER	*You pick out a single negative detail and dwell on it exclusively so that your vision of all reality becomes darkened. "I shouldn't have cut that person off. I'm a bad driver."*

ALL-OR-NOTHING THINKING	*You see things in black and white and don't allow yourself to see exceptions to the rule. "Because of that one slip, the whole production was a failure."*
LABELING/MISLABELING	*This is an extreme form of over-generalization. Instead of describing your error, you attach a negative label to yourself: "I'm a loser." Mislabeling involves describing an event with language that is highly colored and emotionally loaded.*
EMOTIONAL REASONING	*You assume that your negative emotions reflect the way things really are: "I feel stupid, so I must be so stupid."*
DISQUALIFYING THE POSITIVE	*You reject positive experiences by insisting they "don't count" for some reason or other. In this way you can maintain a negative belief that is contradicted by your everyday experiences. "I only got the job because Brad's father put in a good word for me."*

4. TIME OUT

The time out technique is a contract made between families, friends, or co-workers. It acknowledges that anyone can lose control of their anger and be tempted to do or say hurtful things. As a result, proactive measures are taken to avoid any verbal or physical assaults by leaving the scene and returning when it is safe. When explaining Time Out to family and friends, be sure to emphasize that you are using this technique because you no longer wish to hurt people with your words or behavior. Be sure to let them know it is a loving act towards them.

There are five stages in time-out, and they are known as the Five R's—**R**ecognition, **R**esistance, **R**emoval, **R**efocus, and **R**eturn.

- **Recognition** is recognizing those cues that tell us our anger is escalating. This includes our physical, behavioral, cognitive, and emotional signs. When we recognize these angry symptoms, they are a warning that we need to exit.
- **Resistance** is the ability to resist offending someone as we plan an escape route. Our goal is to resist throwing back insults, uttering words beneath our breath, and thinking hostile thoughts as we prepare to leave.
- **Removal** is the ability to physically remove ourselves from the scene and go to a place where we can be alone to think.
- **Refocusing** allows us to shift from fight mode to think mode and to evaluate what we want from the situation. Refocusing allows us to be more grounded and less emotional as we evaluate what truly matters most.
- **Return** is the decision to return in order to talk things out amicably. A commitment to be back at a certain time period should be honored. Upon return, we should be cautious not to get caught up in another cycle of conflict, and focus our efforts on solving the problem.

Why Is Time Out Critical?

Time out is critical because very little can be accomplished when two parties are heated. Our fight- or-flight response can trigger us to become irrational and unpredictable resulting in us saying and doing things we later regret. If our goal is to problem solve, we need to do so when we can be calm and in control of our emotions and our behavior.

5. FAIR FIGHTING RULES

Fair fighting rules are the ten commandments of a relationship. They pertain to the limits of what we can do and say when we are trying to problem solve. Fair fighting rules keep the exchange fair and decrease opportunities for parties involved to hit below the belt. They also keep us accountable when we fail to follow these rules. Below are some suggested rules. You can also add on to this list or create your own.

DO'S	DON'TS
Tell people how you feel.	No hitting, pushing, shoving or threatening to do so
Take time outs as needed.	No attacking the person
Be respectful.	No wishing/fantasizing evil
Actively listen.	No bringing up the past
Seek solutions.	No controlling behavior
Sit down and talk.	No punishing with silence
Be engaging.	No ganging up
Be open-minded.	No standing up and yelling
Talk about the issues at hand.	No running away, ignoring or denying issues
Be conscious of body language	No provoking others with bodily gestures

6. ANGER LADDER

This technique requires us to gauge our anger level by mentally plotting it on a numerical scale from 0-10 (0 representing calm and 10 representing rage). Ideally, we should be able to quickly retrieve and identify this information habitually. For example, a 2 might represent a situation in which we realize we left our important documents at the office, and a 9 might be when our partner embarrasses us in front of the children.

The ladder provides suggestions to follow when we find ourselves at a particular number on the scale during conflict.

Notice, we do very little problem-solving beyond #5. That is why it is critical you monitor your anger throughout the day. Past 5, your fight-or-flight kicks in, and any attempt to resolve will result in chaos!

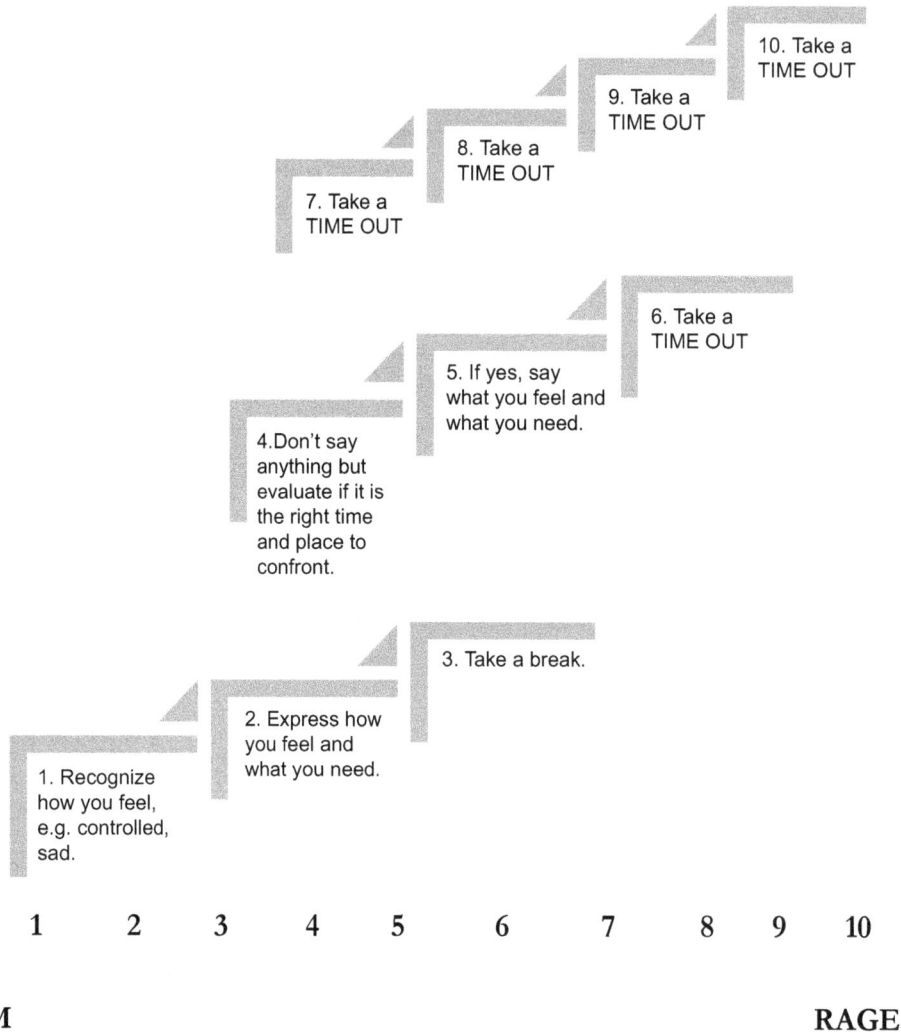

10. Take a TIME OUT

9. Take a TIME OUT

8. Take a TIME OUT

7. Take a TIME OUT

6. Take a TIME OUT

5. If yes, say what you feel and what you need.

4.Don't say anything but evaluate if it is the right time and place to confront.

3. Take a break.

2. Express how you feel and what you need.

1. Recognize how you feel, e.g. controlled, sad.

| 0 | 1 | 2 | 3 | 4 | 5 | 6 | 7 | 8 | 9 | 10 |

CALM   **RAGE**

7. ASSERTIVENESS

Assertiveness is communicating in a fashion that demonstrates respect for our self and others. Assertiveness is confronting others lovingly but truthfully. Without honestly disclosing the contents of our heart to those who offend us, our primary feelings stay suppressed and our anger expresses itself without permission in unhealthy ways.

Assertive expression is a task we must learn if we want to manage our anger and negative emotions. Talking is instinctive for most of us, so we take it for granted. However, words and their delivery have a lot of power, and can be misused. Words have the power to lift someone up or tear someone down. Thus, learning to communicate effectively is an important key to mastering our anger and deescalating the anger of others.

The end result of an assertive experience should leave the messenger feeling validated and authentic and the receiver feeling informed. This is done through an "I Statement." An "I Statement" includes all the elements involved in communicating assertively. To do this, we must

1. Initiate all communication with the word "I." This is in contrast to the word "You" which tends to make people feel blamed. E.g., "You are ...." vs. "I felt extremely...."
2. Insert the word "feel" or "felt" in all your statements. Do not use alternatives such as "think" or "know." What we feel is not debatable; what we think is.
3. Express only primary emotions, e.g., controlled, disrespected. (Do not use the emotion of anger or any of its synonyms like upset, mad, livid etc. when communicating)
4. Focus on the behavior that is problematic rather than someone's character or personality.
   E.g. coming home late, taking property.
5. Tell them what you need in the future.
   E.g., "I felt disrespected when you came home late last night. I would like you to call next time if you will be late."

From being assertive, we discover the position of the other person and find answers to questions such as:

1. Do they know they are hurting me?
2. Do they care they are hurting me?
3. Are they willing to stop hurting me?
    FYI (*If someone does not care about our feelings, we need to make some decisions about that relationship*)

The answers to these three questions are critical because they empower us to make decisions about what we want to do about the relationship. They allow us to separate fact from fiction by giving us details and clarity about the other person's position.

8. FOLLOW THROUGH

Once we communicate assertively, we must follow through on securing what we need from that person. Boundaries on acceptable behavior must be laid out, and what our intentions are if these boundaries are crossed. When we fail to follow through on our intentions, it sends very strong messages that we don't respect ourselves or our own boundaries. We lose credibility, and our lack of follow-through says, "It is okay for others to hurt me."

The concept of follow-through is even important with athletes. Sports like basketball and swimming require the athletes to keep the pace at which they start. A swimmer who starts quickly but cannot maintain stamina will likely not flourish. It is the same underlying belief when it comes to our emotional well-being. We must maintain our stand on what we will and will not accept from others.

In order to follow through effectively, it is suggested:

a) We have clear boundaries about what we need from the other person.
b) We communicate our intentions if boundaries are crossed. Include specific details so the other person is also clear, e.g., "If my needs for respect are not met in this way…I'll have to…" Do not promise to do something if you are not willing to follow through.

c) Be attentive so that you notice signs of their cooperation.

d) Encourage and affirm the other person when we see positive change.

e) Respectively communicate once you notice boundaries have been crossed.

f) Receive feedback about their actions.

g) Follow through with your intentions.

9. DIAPHRAGMATIC BREATHING

When you look at a baby sleeping, you will notice as they breathe that their stomach moves up and down. Babies, in their most content and relaxed state, breathe from their diaphragms—not their chests. Most of us have forgotten how to breathe properly. Diaphragmatic breathing is effectively used to allow the body to function at its optimum level. To practice diaphragmatic breathing, follow these instructions:

Find yourself in a comfortable position. You can sit on a chair, lie on the floor, or anywhere you find yourself. Your diaphragm is a large muscle beneath your lungs. Once you take your first breath, your lungs will be expanded, and it will press down on your diaphragm, and consequently, your abdomen too will expand as your lungs get filled with air.

Some people prefer to close their eyes or just focus on a fixed object. Do which ever you please.

1. Start by examining your entire body for tension. Meditate and pay attention to your body, and sense where you might be feeling anger, tightness, or discomfort. Scan your entire body starting from the top of your head to the soles of your feet.

2. Put one hand on your chest and the other hand on your diaphragm. When you start to breath, make sure the hand on your diaphragm rises higher than the hand on your chest.

3. Exhale completely, and then inhale taking slow deep breaths through your nose. Imagine you are sucking all the air in the room and hold it for a count of five. Exhale again, counting down slowly from five. Notice the tension you may be having in various parts of the body at this time.

4. Once again, take a deep breath. Notice how your breath enters and leaves your body. Observe your body relaxing and taking in new breaths. Notice your level of relaxation.

5. Take in another deep breath through your nose. Again, imagine you are sucking all the air in the room and count to five. Exhale again, counting down from five. Pay attention to your hand on your diaphragm and your chest.

6. Take three more full breaths. Fill your lungs and chest with air. Be conscious of the bodily changes and the state of your relaxation. Use your breathing to cleanse away all your tiredness, anger, resentment, and anxiety you may have felt through-out the day.

7. In silence, come to a close and take a final breath. Open your eyes and contemplate how different you feel.

You can practice this exercise twice a day or when you find yourself fixated on angry or upsetting thoughts.

10. SELF-CARE/BALANCE

It is important we take time out to replenish ourselves because our days can be filled with stress and emotional battles. Making sure we have had enough time with ourselves to handle the onslaught of triggers is very important. Self-care requires taking proactive measures to love our self. It includes taking care of our physical, emotional, psychological, and spiritual health. It puts a plan in place to avoid burnout and a feeling of weariness. Self-care also sends a strong message that you respect and value yourself. When we take care of our self, we are stronger, wiser, and more capable of taking care of others. When we don't replenish lost energy, we don't have much to give to those we are responsible for.

Time Alone

Times of quietness allow us the luxury of being away from the chaos of our everyday life. We are able to hear ourselves think and are more receptive to our own solutions. Only when we are alone can we slip into a state of quiet meditation, and allow our problems to work themselves out in our subconscious.

Relaxation

Giving our body some special treatment is a natural way to relieve stress. Other than keeping our skin soft and our bodies in good repair, spa-related activities like massages and warm baths have been known to soothe even small colicky babies like nothing else. Such activities continue to be effective tools for relaxation as we get older, but we sometimes forget to utilize them. Taking a break amidst a tub of warm bubbles or under the warm hands of an experienced masseuse can help us feel like we are escaping a stressful reality and taking a mental and emotional vacation. It triggers the relaxation response which allows us to come back to the reality of our life feeling refreshed and relaxed.

Physical Exercise/Stretching

Many of us experience emotional stress through our body by way of psychosomatic symptoms. Because we are very vulnerable to emotional problems, it is important we take care of our physical strength through exercise and stretching. When we exercise, our brain releases endorphins, adrenaline, serotonin, and dopamine. These chemicals all work together to make us experience positive feelings. In addition, exercising allows our muscles to relax, easing tension and strain.

11. CHOOSING YOUR BATTLES

Focus on what is right, not who is right.

Make decisions based on what is right, not who is right. We can get caught up in winning the battle and lose sight of the problem that really needs to be resolved. Great maturity is needed to focus on solutions and not victories or defeats.

Prioritize what is meaningful.

Life is filled with opportunities to choose between making a big deal out of something and simply letting it go. We will need to reevaluate our priorities and turn away those battles that are not meaningful to us. When we fight every battle, we are not taken seriously on issues that are really personal and consequential.

Mind your own business.

Ideally, each of us would like to live a peaceful, tranquil, relatively stress-free life. To do this, we need to stay within our personal space of personal concerns. We need to stay out of those areas that are not our business and those that we cannot do anything about.

Don't try to change people

Though we may have the best of intentions, we can find ourselves trying to change people's belief systems or personalities. People fight back hard when they recognize this. We cannot change people. Real lasting change comes from personal realization and inner determination. It is advisable not to focus our battles on trying to change people.

MARIA'S STORY

Maria grew up in a home with an alcoholic mother. She remembers being left alone as early as five years old. Even though her family did not struggle financially, she always yearned for her mother's attention, which was rarely available. As a teenager, Maria would rebel, often against her mother who was now sober. Maria would call her mother names, and would even attempt to physically hit her. She rebelled, hung out with the wrong crowd, and would continue to have a rocky but dependent relationship with her mother over the years.

Maria ended up having a set of twins with her husband who was a successful businessman. They could want for nothing. They lived in an affluent neighborhood, drove top-of-the-line cars, and could literally afford anything money could buy. Yet, Maria felt empty, and would turn to alcohol to sooth the emptiness. Her full-time nanny would be the one to care for the children the majority of the time. Maria's husband resented Maria's neglect of their children. They had chosen to have the children, and they agreed that she would be a stay-at-home mother. He could not understand why Maria couldn't stay sober.

Corporate parties were especially embarrassing for him. Maria would out-drink everybody in the room, and he would often have to carry her out on his shoulder. Time and time again, he threatened to leave her if she did not change her ways. Maria would hide and sneak around in order to drink.

In counseling sessions with Maria, she spoke sadly of early memories of having to watch her mother pass out on the couch as she rocked herself to sleep. She remembers having to wake up in the morning to get to school and having no one to supervise her. She revealed that she found child- rearing difficult and that the emotional responsibilities of the children were over-whelming. She could not confide in her husband about her fears and insecurities because she feared his judgment. Ultimately, the opportunity to share this pain with him proved fruitful. She was able to see that she had very little familiarity with taking care of people and being taken care of because she had been neglected. Her lack of familiarity with caring for others triggered her fears and anxiety, and she used alcohol to self-medicate. Maria's pursuit of forgiveness towards her mother was a journey she felt she had to undergo in order to tackle her responsibilities as a mother.

Suggested Activities

1. Emotional Needs Chart
2. Time Out
3. Anger Ladder
4. Learning Assertiveness

ACCOUNT STATEMENT

MONTH_____

Anger Item	Date	Cost
E.g., Raised my voice	March 13	50
1.		
2.		
3.		
4.		
5.		
6.		
7.		
8.		
9.		
10.		
11.		
12.		
13.		

14.		
15.		
16.		
17.		
18.		
19.		
20.		
21.		
22.		
23.		
24.		
25.		
26.		
27.		
28.		

Total: _____

EMOTIONAL NEEDS CHART

Support Person	Relationship	Emotional Need	Back-up Plan

Notes to Self:

_____

_____

_____

_____

_____

TIME OUT

Please, write out your plan for occasions where your pride or some other reason might get in the way of you taking a time out. For each of your possible objections, write a rebuttal that would motivate you to take a time out anyway.

E.g.

Objection: *It's my house, why do I have to leave!*

Rebuttal: *If I don't leave, I may lose more than my house!*

Objection: _____

Rebuttal:_____

Objection: _____

Rebuttal:_____

Objection: _____

Rebuttal:_____

Objection: _____

Rebuttal:_____

ANGER LADDER

A simple way to monitor your anger is to use an Anger Ladder. A score of 0 means calm, and a score of 10 means rage—a point on your spectrum when you have lost control. For the next six weeks, record how high you get on your anger ladder.

Monday	Tuesday	Wednesday	Thursday	Friday	Saturday	Sunday
Week 1						
Week 2						
Week 3						
Week 4						
Week 5						
Week 6						

Start Date _____   Sign_____

WORKSHEET #1

Use this sheet for each week that you are monitoring.

1) What was the highest number you reached on the anger ladder during the past week?

2) What was the event that triggered your anger?

3) What cues were associated with the anger-provoking event?
   Physical cues_____
   Behavioral cues_____
   Emotional cues_____
   Cognitive cues _____

Notes:

_____
_____
_____
_____
_____
_____
_____
_____
_____

Week Date _____   Sign _____

WORKSHEET #2

Use this sheet for each week that you are monitoring.

1) What was the highest number you reached on the anger ladder during the past week?

2) What was the event that triggered your anger?

3) What cues were associated with the anger-provoking event?
   Physical cues _____
   Behavioral cues _____
   Emotional cues _____
   Cognitive cues _____

Notes:

_____
_____
_____
_____
_____
_____
_____
_____

Week Date _____   Sign_____

WORKSHEET #3

Use this sheet for each week that you are monitoring.

1) What was the highest number you reached on the anger ladder during the past week?

2) What was the event that triggered your anger?

3) What cues were associated with the anger-provoking event?
Physical cues_____
Behavioral cues_____
Emotional cues_____
Cognitive cues _____

Notes:

_____
_____
_____
_____
_____
_____
_____
_____

Week Date _____ Sign_____

WORKSHEET #4

Use this sheet for each week that you are monitoring.

1) What was the highest number you reached on the anger ladder during the past week?

2) What was the event that triggered your anger?

3) What cues were associated with the anger-provoking event?
    Physical cues_____
    Behavioral cues_____
    Emotional cues_____
    Cognitive cues _____

Notes:

_____
_____
_____
_____
_____
_____
_____
_____

Week Date _____   Sign_____

WORKSHEET #5

Use this sheet for each week that you are monitoring.

1) What was the highest number you reached on the anger ladder during the past week?

2) What was the event that triggered your anger?

3) What cues were associated with the anger-provoking event?
   Physical cues_____
   Behavioral cues_____
   Emotional cues_____
   Cognitive cues _____

Notes:

_____
_____
_____
_____
_____
_____
_____
_____
_____

Week Date _____   Sign _____

WORKSHEET #6

Use this sheet for each week that you are monitoring.

1) What was the highest number you reached on the anger ladder during the past week?

2) What was the event that triggered your anger?

3) What cues were associated with the anger-provoking event?
   Physical cues_____
   Behavioral cues_____
   Emotional cues_____
   Cognitive cues _____

Notes:

_____
_____
_____
_____
_____
_____
_____
_____

Week Date _____   Sign _____

LEARNING ASSERTIVENESS

Review and write about two recent situations where you could have been assertive.

First Scenario

What did the person do or fail to do that hurt you? Explain.

_____

_____

What are the feelings you had when the person hurt you?

_____

_____

What is the specific act or behavior you did not like?

_____

_____

Provide your "I statement." E.g., *"I felt disrespected when you did not call me last night. I would like you to call me next time."*

_____

_____

Second Scenario

What did the person do or fail to do that hurt you? Explain.

_____

_____

What are the feelings you had when the person hurt you?

_____

_____

What is the specific act or behavior you did not like?

_____

_____

Provide your "I statement."

Chapter 4

DEBT FORGIVENESS

Debt Forgiveness goes beyond managing debt; it absolves an individual from all debt, including retroactively cancelling all previous debt an individual is unable to pay. As a result, that individual is forgiven and is no longer required to pay back any overdue funds.

When we have unresolved pain from our past or live in difficult relationships, forgiveness can be the option that frees us from the torture of holding onto anger and suffering continuously.

This chapter will address forgiveness, and the steps we can take to rid ourselves of resentment as well as hatred.

GIVING UP HATRED

Hatred is an enduring attitude or sentiment towards a person manifested by anger, aversion and desire for the person's misfortune. It is the result of judging someone as bad, evil and unforgivable. Hatred is fully committed to thoughts and behaviors that seek to hurt and punish those who have hurt us.

Hatred is the result of unresolved emotional pain consuming an individual. Eventually, the person's character becomes full of hate. When we reach the point of hating, we fail to realize we become the vessel in which that hatred resides and a victim to its destructive venom. We become blind to hatred's tendency to strip us of all the good in our life, destroying our relationships, opportunities and our personality. The hatred of even one person has the power to singlehandedly destroy every other relationship in our life.

Shame can be associated with hating someone close to us, especially a family member. As a result, we don't communicate our pain and consequently we live with this hatred and suffer.

Hatred possesses ill will towards others and includes the tendency to:

- Put personal needs before everyone else.
- Be distrustful about sharing details of our feelings and inner conflict with others.

Hatred is directing our unresolved anger at ourselves and others.

GIVING UP RESENTMENT

Resentment is "bitter indignation at having been treated unfairly." When those we care about hurt us in some fashion and we are unable to communicate our pain or resolve our hurt, it lives in us as resentment. We live with discontentment and hold on to the anger in fear of jeopardizing the relationship.

Unspoken pain or unresolved hurt compromises our quality of life. Because it is a personal and private emotion, we feel the brunt of these painful feelings. We are unable to enjoy life at its fullest because misery accompanies this secret pain.

When we resent, we hold the keys to our freedom in spite of our choice not to use it. Among the reasons why we don't express our feelings include fear of rejection, a sense of hopelessness in successfully resolving the problem, ineffective communication skills and a host of other reasons. However, when we make the choice not to communicate, resentment takes up permanent residence within us, and we live with our misery perpetually.

Resentment can have the following characteristics:

1. **Passive Resentment** is the tendency to neglect ourselves. We treat ourselves as second-class citizens and deny ourselves due attention and care. Instead, we direct our care toward others(often our spouses, children or friends), and neglect our own needs, be it aesthetic, career, social, medical, etc. We become a punching bag for life and other people.

2. **Aggressive Resentment** is the tendency to abuse ourselves. Our abusive nature may include the use of substances such as alcohol or recreational drugs or even abuse against the body like sex outside of its proper boundaries. We sabotage relationships and work opportunities and live in fear based relationships because of our abusive nature.

3. **Passive-Aggressive Resentment** is the tendency to overly control ourselves. We maintain control in everything including our finances, relationships, home, etc. We carry the burden of everyone around us and fail to enjoy our own lives. We feel like if we stop controlling our lives, everything will fall apart. Unfortunately, we never really end up living because we spend most of our energy playing God.

Ultimately, resentment is directing our unresolved anger at ourselves!

APPLYING FORGIVENESS

Forgiveness can be a struggle for many of us because we confuse it with other terms which do not empower us. For this reason, before we can discuss the specifics of forgiveness, we need to discuss what it is not.

1. Forgiveness is not forgetting.

The popular saying "Forgive and forget" seems to be quoted when people are trying to encourage each other. However, this saying is incorrect because it fails to validate the feelings of the one hurting. Forgiveness is not forgetting. In fact, I propose the following " to forgive and remember."

- **Remember** the freedom you find in letting your anger, resentment,and hatred go.
- **Remember** the hope you find in yourself and others when you can see more clearly.
- **Remember** to never let hatred control you ever again.

2. Forgiveness is not reconciling.

Many people do not forgive because they think if they do, they must let those who hurt them back in their lives again. This is not true. It is important to understand there are behaviors and experiences that are destructive to our emotional health, and it is unwise to put ourselves back in a relationship that tempts us to resent or hate. It would be self-sabotaging and ultimately our downfall if we should welcome someone back into our life who hasn't proven him/herself to be protective with our trust and our love. It is absolutely necessary to thoroughly test for genuinely changed behavior—if you decide to reconcile. However, we can still forgive even if it is not possible to reconcile.

3. Forgiveness is not pardoning.

If a judicial system has taken over or a third party has become involved, forgiveness does not prevent any sort of corrective discipline punishment from taking place. In fact, forgiveness recognizes that some of the best emotional and spiritual growth comes from times when we are going through a reprimand of some kind. It can be a time of self-reflection and inner healing.

4. Forgiveness is not excusing.

Forgiveness does not try to justify behavior. No matter how difficult life has been for someone, it does not justify that person's hurtful behavior towards us. Forgiveness recognizes the act committed was hurtful and does not try to defend or find excuses for harmful behavior.

FORGIVENESS

Forgiveness is a conscious decision to let go of resentment or hatred we have towards someone.

Forgiveness hurts!

Resentment and hatred is like stepping on broken glass. Just like the glass hurt going into your foot, it will hurt coming out. This can be said of emotional pain being released. As we play out the painful memories, we will be confronted with the magnitude of our pain. At times, it may feel like we are falling apart, but the goal is to stay faithful to the process.

THE FORGIVENESS PROCESS

Forgiveness takes place in two stages.

A. The first stage is a mental process of deciding to forgive.
B. The second stage is an emotional process of feeling the pain being released through the remembrance of the offense.

When we start the forgiveness process, the following steps are recommended:

1. Go to a safe place where you can think in quietness.
2. Perform some type of ceremony to represent the actual act of letting go (like flushing a toilet, washing your hands, or releasing a balloon into the sky).
3. Vocalize outwardly, "I forgive you," referring to the person with whom you are angry.

4. Once a commitment has been made, your emotions will start to release. You will experience pain.

5. Stay present as your emotions direct you to cry, to wail and to grieve. Allow yourself to be comforted.

6. Don't run away, mask, or control painful feelings such as shame, injustice, anger, or sadness.

7. When you wake up the second day, repeat this process again.

8. Repeat this act for a total of seven days.

After the seventh day, continue to forgive every time a memory presents itself by simply responding to the pain with the words, "I forgive you."

As long as memories present themselves, we need to continue forgiving. As time goes on, the memories should be fewer and fewer, until you reach a point where they cease altogether.

The Knowing

Like all wounds, when our hurt has been healed, it looks different and feels different. When we have really captured the essence of forgiveness, we will be able to still remember the offense that took place (e.g., the fact that you were abandoned); however, the feelings that once accompanied the memories no longer remain. For instance, consider a physical wound that happened in your childhood, like falling off your bike. Take a good look at that wound now. Do you remember the events that took place? Does it still hurt? So it is with forgiveness! We remember, but we don't hurt anymore.

Compassion

When we can see the offender as wounded and possibly a prisoner of their own past pain, we may start to feel empathy for that person rather than resent or hate him/her. We may even become willing to share the pain in their life. This is compassion, and that compassion comes from the heart. When we have compassion, we see the other in a loving, understanding way versus a condemning way. We see the person as a human being. All human beings are worthy of respect—not because of their failings—but in spite of them.

Confession/Shame

Confession is critical in healing. Once we are able to communicate our pain to someone we trust, our healing can be manifested. When we come face-to-face with our pain, it is very probable that we start to experience shame about the occurrence or even shame that we held onto it. Regardless, we will have to actively deal with shame. The following points identify some steps we can take:

1. Come out of hiding and have the courage to say, "Here I am¼."

Declare yourself to another person. It is important to choose a safe person and a safe place. Make sure the person you declare yourself to is a faithful, mature person, e.g., a trusted and proven friend or a professional counselor.

2. We admit, "I am naked."

We admit to God, to ourselves, and to another human being the exact nature of what happened. Acknowledging the presence of an enemy is the only way to defeat it. Our greatest enemy is our self. Acknowledging one's weakness, problem, or fear of being exposed is always the first step to overcoming it.

Affirm

Someone has said, "I know there is a God, and I know I am not HIM." The journey of becoming fully human begins with the thorough acceptance of our humanity. Some affirmations we can meditate on include:

- There is nothing that I have done or haven't done that can make me less than anyone else.
- I am just as important as everyone else. I have value and God loves me.

If we hear our shaming tapes inside our mind installed by our parents, others, or our own perfectionism dismissing our statement, say it again and again, louder and louder, until it gets inside us. Let truth set us free!

Move towards Others

Join the human race, accepting your need for community. Give yourself permission to be human. Let go of the entrenched cover-ups to hide your mistakes through perfectionism, work-a-holism, criticism, control, and blame.

Ways I can move toward others

- Join a group.
- Become more socially involved.
- Invite people over.
- Invite others to share your day.
- Go out with people from work.
- Say hello to as many people today as you can.
- Volunteer.
- Go to church.
- Talk to people at the checkout counter.
- Go to a sporting event.
- Start a hobby.

Experience the positive regard of others

Self-acceptance experienced through the loving, positive regard from God and others helps overcome toxic shame. It is your human existence which qualifies you to be respected and valued. It is like having citizenship. If you are an American, you have certain rights that others may not have. If you belong to the human race, I want to tell you that you deserve to love and to be loved. Find yourself relationships where you can experience the positive regard of others. However, work hard at also giving what you need. Give to others that same positive regard—no matter what they have or haven't done.

Self Reflection/Asking Forgiveness From Others

Start to reflect on how your resentment or hatred has affected those close to you.

1. Become conscious of your past actions as well as those individuals you may have hurt.
2. Ask them for their forgiveness.
3. Receive their forgiveness and declare to yourself, "I am forgiven!"

Surrender Every Hateful Thought

Moving forward, become conscious of all thoughts that have hatred attached to them on a daily basis. For instance, fleeting thoughts that may have one time been acceptable such as generalizations or stereotypes. E.g. "I hate hypocrites or "I hate my hair. Capture every thought that hatred has aligned itself with and surrender it to God. Your goal is to rid yourself of the word" hate" in your psyche. Once hatred has been totally defeated from your mind, you will start to experience new relationships with everyone and everything.

Put A Plan In Place

1. Inquire into who is willing and able to have a healthy relationship with you. This includes your support network of family, friends, and colleagues.
2. Evaluate if there is anyone in your life with whom you may have to temporarily pull away from until he/she is emotional healthy. You do not want to get pulled into resenting or hating again.
3. Live life accordingly

TODD'S STORY

Todd and his two sisters grew up with their mother and father. When Todd was younger, he travelled with his mom to Europe for vacations. He recalled seeing his mom being embraced by a man on one occasion and even kissing him on another. His mom would refer to this man as her friend, but Todd was always suspicious. When they got home, his father would often ask him how he enjoyed his trip, and he would not disclose very much information. These questionable occurrences continued to happen until he was fourteen, when he stopped vacationing with his mother. He never spoke to his mother about the events he witnessed.

By his early thirties Todd had built a moving company from scratch. He was very good at managing money. At the height of his success, he met a young lady who worked nights at a restaurant, and he fell madly in love with her. When they first met, she explained that she was only waitressing because she had acquired a lot of debt that she needed to pay off. He was so in love with her that he offered to manage her money and help her out. This arrangement would also give him an opportunity to keep an eye on her.

However, as time persisted, Todd grew more and more suspicious of her behavior and started becoming paranoid every time she failed to account for her whereabouts. Even though she would always provide ample evidence, he would become consumed with jealousy and rage. He had keys to her apartment, but he would be consistently paranoid.

In counseling, he acknowledged great fear in contemplating his mom's potential infidelity. He did not want to see his mother in that light. He knew he would have to partake in a candid heart-to- heart with his mother in order to rid himself of his distrust towards women in general. He had seen this pattern of distrust in all his relationships and started to realize that it may have stemmed from these unresolved fears of his mother's infidelity he had as a child.

Suggested Activities

1. Shame Inventory
2. Reflection Exercise
3. Resentment Questionnaire
4. Forgiveness Exercise # 1
5. Forgiveness Exercise #2

ACCOUNT STATEMENT

MONTH_____

Anger Item	Date	Cost
E.g., Raised my voice	March 13	50
1.		
2.		
3.		
4.		
5.		
6.		
7.		
8.		
9.		
10.		
11.		
12.		
13.		
14.		
15.		
16.		
17.		
18.		
19.		

20.		
21.		
22.		
23.		
24.		
25.		
26.		
27.		
28.		

Total: _____

SHAME INVENTORY

Check the boxes below if they often pertain to you.

Add your checkmarks and record your total in the blank provided at the end of the page.

- ☐   I feel uncomfortable when others are having fun.
- ☐   I feel guilty or ashamed if I am hurt.
- ☐   I withdraw from others when I get hurt or angry.
- ☐   I often feel like "I will never be good enough."
- ☐   I feel ashamed if I fail at something.
- ☐   I have parts of my life story I have never told anyone.
- ☐   I feel embarrassed or ashamed of enjoying or celebrating my sexuality.
- ☐   I become defensive whenever questioned.
- ☐   I struggle with celebrating my successes.
- ☐   I feel ashamed of being angry.
- ☐   I feel ashamed if I am lonely.

☐   I tend to criticize and judge others.

☐   I tend get depressed if someone criticizes me.

☐   I tend to get anxious in new social situations.

☐   I tend to be secretive or very private.

☐   I feel ashamed to be afraid.

☐   I tell half-truths.

☐   I feel ashamed for how others have treated me.

☐   I feel like something is wrong with me.

☐   I pretend like I am happy, but I am often unhappy.

Total: _____

Score Ratings:

1-5   You sometimes struggle with toxic shame.

5-10   You should continue to work on your assertiveness.

10-15   You are struggling with toxic shame and would be wise to assertively address the issues.

16-20   Begin working on your toxic shame issues NOW!

REFLECTION EXERCISE

Stand in front of a mirror. Now, look at your face.

Ask yourself, "What do you think of this person?" Look at your body. Look into your mind. See into your heart.

Where do your thoughts take you? Are they critical, judgmental or nurturing? What are you feeling? What are your feelings about yourself?

The rejection of self is central to shame. In order to counter negative feelings about yourself, you must make a decision to love yourself unconditionally. Go ahead and say it out loud.

"Today, I will decide to love myself unconditionally."

Say it again a little more assertively.

"Today, I will decide to love myself unconditionally."

Say it again louder.

"Today, I will decide to love myself unconditionally."

Now can you ask yourself, "Will I love myself no matter what I do or don't do?"

Will you do for yourself what you want others to do for you?

RESENTMENT QUESTIONNAIRE

Consider the relationship that is causing the most anger, resentment or hate and answer the following questions:

I really hate the way you _____

_____

I have blamed you for _____

_____

It makes me feel sad when I think of _____

_____

All I ever wanted was _____

_____

But all I ever got was _____

_____

I get so angry with you because _____

_____

Why do you always have to_____

_____

Why can't you just once _____

_____

I still carry a lot of hurt inside because_____

My biggest fear used to be _____

_____

I am probably going to hold on to my resentment until you_____

_____

What I may have to change about me so I can go on with my life is

_____

My greatest wish for you in the future is_____

_____

My greatest wish for myself in the future is _____

_____

My biggest fear today is _____

_____

I still feel some guilt because _____

_____

Sometimes I still feel some shame for _____

_____

FORGIVENESS EXERCISE #1

You will need a pencil, a journal, and a symbol of your hatred. Please understand that you may feel uncomfortable, but we recommend you make a firm commitment to proceed until you complete the entire process.

Create a list of people you are angry with, resent or hate.
Write down a list of all the individuals in your life you can still recall that you have unresolved emotional issues with. You may have simply buried it or denied it but try to pull it out.

1. **Forgive each individual in your mind and confess or declare it with your mouth.**
    On a scale from 0-10, with 10 being most intense, rate your resentment or hatred toward this person. Imagine that person's face in your mind and recall the experience of your hurt. Say to that person, "I forgive you."

2. **Journal.**
    Put into your journal the following statement:
    I forgive *insert name of person* and release *name the pain and hurt caused.*

3. After you completely forgive that person in your mind, document how you feel and all the subsequent emotions that surface throughout your days and weeks.

4. **Express gratitude.**
    Give thanks to God for holding onto you through this process and for giving you the strength to endure through the good and bad days during the process.

5. **Repeat.**
    Repeat this with the same person for seven days before moving on to the next person.

6. **Reassess.**
    After the seventh day, assess your hatred on your scale from 1-10.

FORGIVENESS EXERCISE #2

When you have some comfort level and feel able to go beyond Forgiveness Exercise #1, proceed to do the following:

1. **Relax.**

   Go to a safe place in your home—a quiet place where you won't be disturbed. Take some deep breaths and recognize any tension. Breathe to eliminate the tension.

2. **Recall and ask questions.**

   Bring to memory the individual you forgave in Step 1. Try to think of what type of life that person has. Consider the various variables that could have affected the way that individual related to people. If you do not know, ask yourself, "Did he/she have abusive parents? Did he/she undergo trauma?" If you had lived that person's life, ask yourself, "Would I be any different?"

3. **Empathize.**

   Relate to the person's possible brokenness and ignorance of not knowing better. Don't pity him/her, but just try to understand that just as you were a victim of that person's pain, he/she must have been a victim of somebody else's pain. Imagine this person happy and enjoying his/her life. Embrace the belief that your forgiveness has the power to contribute not just to him/her, but his/her children and grandchildren being released from hatred and hateful circumstances. Will you do this for them?

4. **Journal and express.**

   Document how you feel—both good and bad feelings. Don't push away loving thoughts toward that person. Express outwardly, "I no longer hold anything against you". I am free and you are free.

5. **Give gratitude.**

   Express a thank you to God for holding your hand and giving you the strength to get through today and the forgiveness process.

   Repeat this technique for every person on your list.

Chapter 5

SET UP A LOVE ACCOUNT

When we Resolve In-Love Consistently and Habitually, we become rich indeed. Large deposits of love, particularly forgiveness, can be the gateway to emotional freedom and a lasting joy we could have never imagined. When our problem solving techniques have managed to secure us in a safe place away from emotional threats, love offers the building blocks for the relationships that remain we can nurture and truly enjoy.

This final chapter is dedicated to learning how to experience love—our final destination.

MAKE LARGE DEPOSITS OF LOVE

Love is a peculiar word, and there is no shortage of definitions or interpretations of what people think it is. While there are many theories on love, all do agree on the following:

1. Love involves valuing another person's needs and happiness as much as your own. 2. Love involves intimacy and the sharing of thoughts, desires and feelings.

A biblical definition of love discloses that the ingredients of love are patience, kindness, humility, contentedness, forgiveness, respect, self-control, hope, protection, and perseverance in increasing measure.

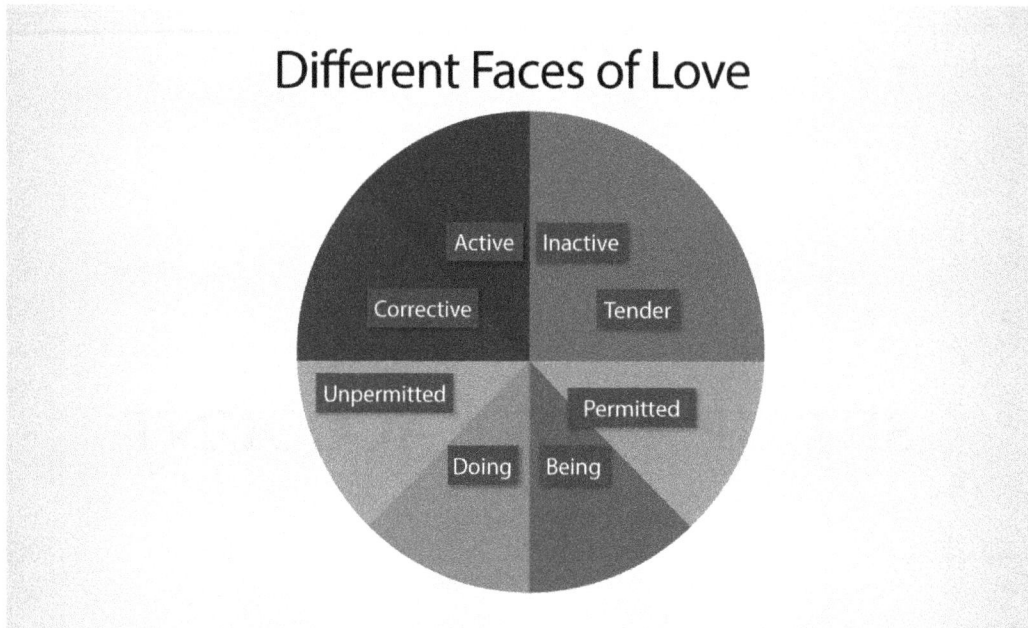

Different Faces of Love

Active | Inactive

Corrective | Tender

Unpermitted | Permitted

Doing | Being

Many people tend to depict love as one-dimensional and associate it exclusively with positive feelings and experiences. However, a more objective evaluation of love will quickly reveal love can be both pleasurable and satisfying and, in the same breath, be painful and heartbreaking. In order to truly experience the totality of love, we need to embrace love as two-dimensional and possessing different faces. Above all, love has an intention of good will towards all people.

RECOGNIZING THE FACES OF LOVE

Tender vs. Corrective

Love can be expressed as tender, warm and yielding—like a mother buying a Popsicle for her son at the park. The word tender can also be described as softhearted, tenderhearted, compassionate, sympathetic, and benevolent. All these words evoke the softer side of love. When love is tender, we experience the gentle side of a person's love.

Love can be corrective or disciplinary when that same mother noted above pulls her son aside to reprimand him for hitting his sister with the Popsicle stick. In this context, love is seen as remedial, therapeutic, restorative, reparative or curative. When love is corrective, we experience the harsher side of a person's love.

Permitted vs. Unpermitted

Love is permitted when we give ourselves permission to receive the love being offered by others and refuse to sabotage relationships and opportunities because of feelings of unworthiness.

Love can be experienced as unpermitted when we don't give ourselves permission to receive love from others or reciprocate it because of feelings of unworthiness. This can be evidenced by the tendency to refuse loving gestures and behaviors from others, and choose to abuse ourselves, our partner, and life's opportunities instead. Often, such individuals are in so much emotional pain, they hurt those they are in relationship with. In these cases, it is not recommended to be in relationship with such individuals until they have worked out their emotional baggage and ceased abusive and destructive tendencies.

Being vs. Doing

Being loved is the act and experience of receiving the love of others, and allowing ourselves the opportunity to embrace all its benefits.

Doing love is the act of expressing and showing love to others in an intentional manner.

Active vs. Inactive

Love is active when we are able to engage in a healthy relationship with a loved one in the "here and now".

Love can be inactive if we are unable to engage in a loving and healthy relationship with someone because they are deceased, unavailable or unable to receive or return that love.

To live successfully as an emotional millionaire requires us to be able to wear these roles whenever necessary. They are all equally loving and powerful demonstrations of love.

ACCESS ALL AVAILABLE SOURCES OF FUNDING

When we feel loved, we can love others; and they can love us in return. This give-and-take quality is what allows love to grow and thrive. However, we must be plugged into a source of love in order to experience and partake in this flowing process.

Sources of Love

Love is always available, but it is our responsibility to place ourselves in situations and to recognize the places, people, and opportunities love is flowing through. Sources of love include:

1. Our support system consists of people including family and friends we trust and whose company we enjoy. A completed needs assessment can help us identify those specific individuals in our lives. Spending time with loved ones should be valued and appreciated.

2. We can also find ourselves reverting back to old patterns of irritability, impatience or carelessness in our current relationships even on a small scale. A great way to increase love is to resist attempts to give into these old behaviors. We can identify and catch these impulses to get angry, resent, or hate, and commit to loving and caring behaviors instead.

3. Spend time visiting and listening to those society has labeled "outcasts" or "hard to love individuals". Often, these individuals are hungry for someone to care and notice them. These individuals could be the black sheep within our own families, in prison, or on the streets. If an opportunity presents itself and if it is safe to do so, take time out to just listen to these individuals and give them an ear.

4. We, ourselves, can also be a source of love when we participate in loving acts towards others. Every single person we meet is a potential lottery ticket because they give us an opportunity to give love so we can create room to receive more love, e.g., being patient with the McDonald's cashier who has made a mistake. As our love radar becomes more and more sensitive, we can detect opportunities to give love and receive love more freely and generously.

5. Love is available in drops and dribbles in the everyday people we come across. We need to be sensitive when others have made themselves a channel to be used of love—even if it's for small things like opening a door or smiling at us. These are loving acts. We need to recognize these messages, be grateful for them and deposit them in our account.

6. Set aside time to specifically pray for those people in your life that have hurt you. This is a powerful and effective way to fill your soul with love. Your prayers should be petitions for their wellbeing and for God to meet their needs.

MAKE LARGE DEPOSITS OF GRATITUDE

Research has recently supported the fact that gratitude is a huge contributor to our mood. Those of us who have previously struggled with anger may have found it difficult to feel grateful when so much of our energy was spent positioning ourselves for conflict. Now that we have been able to successfully utilize problem solving tools to resolve resentful or hateful relationships, we have the remnant of that same energy available to be used for something else. We need to convert that "potential energy" to something useful and positive.

When we want to quit bad habits, we cannot quit cold turkey. We need to replace old habits with new healthier ones. With respect to gratitude, we need to replace old complaining, grumbling and angry thoughts with grateful thoughts all day long.

Learning to be grateful and thinking with gratitude can change our mood immediately. It must become a way of life, and we must practice it daily. The following are some steps we can take to practice making large deposits of gratitude.

1. Keep a gratitude journal.
2. Be conscious of things throughout our day for which we are grateful.
3. Teach those around us the power of gratitude.

GET RICH AND STAY RICH

Having understood the ingredients in love, we all have what it takes to get rich, **R**esolve **I**n-love **C**onsistently and **H**abitually.

If we continue to make large deposits of love, we accumulate wealth indefinitely. When loving becomes routine, we find ourselves full of kindness, patience, respect, forgiveness, humility, good will, hope, faith, and perseverance. When we possess these traits in increasing measure, we feel joy, peace and most of all, freedom.

We have the faith to accomplish our dreams and the passion to enjoy it to the fullest. We finally discover what we were made for, and our lives become meaningful.

REDEEM YOUR SAVINGS

When we have been able to apply the concepts of this book habitually and consistently for at least six months, we have earned permission to fill out the check below giving our selves authority to reap the rewards that follow.

The filling out of this check symbolizes:

- You have fully committed to living a life free of anger, resentment and hate.
- You have fully committed to solving problems promptly and lovingly toward your-self and others.
- You have fully committed to being a forgiving member of society, towards your-self and others.
- You are fully committed to placing Love as the highest priority in your life.

Sign your name in the Payee section and endorse the check before cashing.

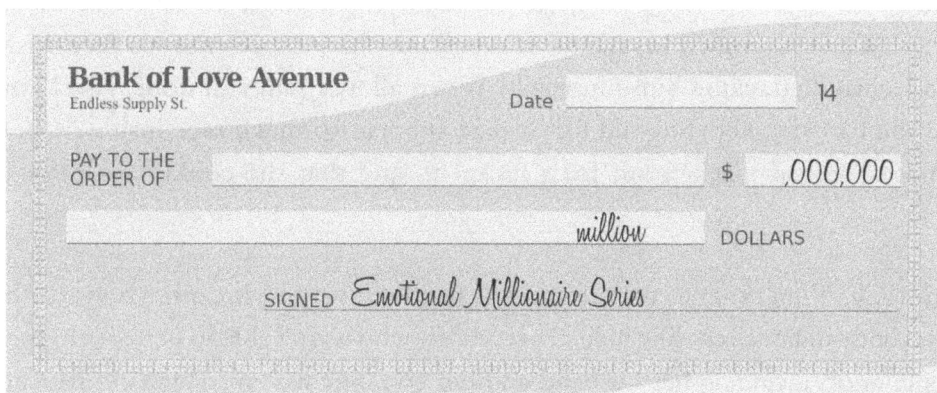

Bank of Love Avenue
Endless Supply St.

Date _____ 14

PAY TO THE
ORDER OF _____ $ *,000,000*

_____ *million* DOLLARS

SIGNED *Emotional Millionaire Series*

Recommendation: Cut out this check below and carry it as a daily reminder of who you have chosen to become. Stay encouraged by it!

NORA'S STORY

Nora grew up in what she would describe as a traditional home. She was always at the top of her class, and her father would constantly put her on a pedestal. She yearned to maintain her daddy's approval in whatever she did. She was completely a daddy's girl.

In her relationships, Nora had to be the one in power, and she would never back down. This frustrated her partner who felt that Nora was too competitive. He would forfeit every battle because Nora would stop at nothing to win. They had an eleven-year-old son who had been diagnosed with ADHD. Nora was consumed with frustration towards her son. Her son drained her energy to the point that she sometimes wished she could abandon him. She couldn't understand why there was such a big difference between him and her eight-year-old daughter, whom Nora perceived as the perfect angel. According to Nora, her daughter listened, earned straight A's and wasn't the least bit rebellious. Nora's husband would complain that her blatant favoritism would cause a rift between the children, but Nora would not have it.

The school would always call Nora to pick up her son for one reason or another. One day, she received yet another call about his acting out, but it was one call too many. She finally had it. When she got to the school, she yelled and screamed at the top of her lungs. When he folded his hands in rebellion, she jumped into his face, lost control, and started attacking him physically. When all was said and done, Nora couldn't believe she had snapped. She did not realize she had so much rage inside of her. She recognized she had blacked out for a moment, and that she could have easily killed him.

In counseling, Nora came to understand she had built very high expectations for herself and everybody in her circle. She judged everybody who wasn't able to perform to her standard as inferior, including her husband and her son. She had absolutely no patience for what she described as mediocrity. She came to understand her early years of outperforming everybody left her insensitive to the creative differences in people. She also realized how she internalized her need to please her own father, and how she had placed that same burden onto her children.

Nora was able to have a conversation with her son and daughter and allow them to know she herself wasn't perfect, but that she had allowed her need for perfection to become a problem.

Suggested Activities

1. Journal how your thoughts, feelings and behaviors have changed since you started your challenge.

ACCOUNT STATEMENT

MONTH_____

Anger Item	Date	Cost
E.g., Raised my voice	March 13	50
1.		
2.		
3.		
4.		
5.		
6.		
7		
8.		
9.		
10.		
11.		
12.		
13.		

14.		
15.		
16.		
17.		
18.		
19.		
20.		
21.		
22.		
23.		
24.		
25.		
26.		
27.		
28.		

Total: _____

JOURNAL

_____

_____

_____

_____

_____

_____

_____

_____

_____

_____

_____

_____

_____

_____

Chapter 6

SPIRITUAL REFERENCES

This section pertains to the Spiritual references that were used to shed light on the recommendations in this book. There is a universal understanding and consensus among these truths that support the benefits of problem solving and forgiveness.

BAHAI FAITH

"Love the creatures for the sake of God and not for themselves. You will never become angry or impatient if you love them for the sake of God. Humanity is not perfect. There are imperfections in every human being, and you will always become unhappy if you look toward the people themselves. But if you look toward God, you will love them and be kind to them, for the world of God is the world of perfection and complete mercy. Therefore, do not look at the shortcomings of anybody; see with the sight of forgiveness."
(Abdu'l-Bahá, *The Promulgation of Universal Peace*, p. 92)

BUDHISM

"He abused me, he struck me, he overcame me, he robbed me' — in those who harbor such thoughts hatred will never cease."

"He abused me, he struck me, he overcame me, he robbed me' — in those who do not harbor such thoughts hatred will cease."
(Dhammapada 1.3-4; trans. Radhakrishnan)

CHRISTIANITY

"Therefore, if you are offering your gift at the altar and there remember that your brother or sisterhas something against you, [24]leave your gift there in front of the altar. First go and be reconciled to them; then come and offer your gift (Mathew 5:23)

"And when you stand praying, if you hold anything against anyone, forgive them, so that your Father in heaven may forgive you your sins." (Mark 11:25)

"If we confess our sins, he is faithful and just and will forgive us our sins and purify us from all unrighteousness. [10]If we claim we have not sinned, we make him out to be a liar and his word is not in us." (1 John 1:9)

JUDAISM

"It is forbidden to be obdurate and not allow yourself to be appeased. On the contrary, one should be easily pacified and find it difficult to become angry. When asked by an offender for forgiveness, one should forgive with a sincere mind and a willing spirit. . . forgiveness is natural to the seed of Israel." (Mishneh Torah, *Teshuvah* 2:10)

HINDUISM

Righteousness is the one highest good; and forgiveness is the one supreme peace; knowledge is one supreme contentment; and benevolence, one sole happiness." (From the Mahabharata, Udyoga Parva Section XXXIII, Translated by Sri Kisari Mohan Ganguli)

ISLAM

Although the just requital for an injustice is an equivalent retribution, those who pardon and maintain righteousness are rewarded by GOD. He does not love the unjust. (Qur'an 42:40).

JANAISM

By practicing *prāyacitta* (repentance), a soul gets rid of sins, and commits no transgressions; he who correctly practices *prāyacitta* gains the road and the reward of the road, he wins the reward of good conduct. By begging forgiveness he obtains happiness of mind; thereby he acquires a kind disposition towards all kinds of living beings; by this kind disposition he obtains purity of character and freedom from fear.
(Māhavīra in *UttarādhyayanaSūtra* 29:17-18)

WORKING REFERENCES

Allan, R. (2006). Getting control of your anger. New York: McGraw-Hill.

Amen, D. (1998). Firestorms in the brain. Fairfield, CA: Mind works Press.

Arlow, B. (1964). Psychoanalytic concepts and the structural theory. NY: International Universities Press.

Averill, J.R. (1982). Studies of anger & aggression - An essay on emotion. New York: Springer Verlag.

Bach, G. R. and Goldberg, H. (1975). Creative aggression - The art of assertive living. New York: Avon Books.

Beck, A. T. et al. (1961). An inventory for measuring depression. Archives of General Psychiatry 4.

Brantley, J. (2007). Calming your anxious mind. San Francisco: Raincoast Books.

Burns, David D. Feeling Good. Morrow, 1980]

Buss, A.H. (1961). The psychology of aggression. New York: John Willey & Sons.

Cannon, W.B. (1989). Stresses and strains of homeostasis. The American Journal of the Medical Sciences 23:120.

Caspi, I.T. et al. (2002). Moving against the world: Life-course patterns of explosive children. Developmental Psychology 23.

Clark H. (2001). A five bar gate. London, United Kingdom: Psychoanalytic Association.

Conger, R (2005). Angry & aggressive behavior across three generations. Journal of Abnormal Child Psychology 31:132-138.

DiGiuseppe, E. et al. (1994). Critical issues in the treatment of anger. Cognitive and Behavioral Practice 1.

Dodge, K. A. (1993). Social cognitive mechanisms in the development of conduct disorder and depression. Annual Review of Psychology, 44, 559-584.

Eagle, M. N. (2007). Psychoanalytic psychology. Psychoanalysis and its Critics 24: 10-24.

Enright, R. & Fitzgibbons, R. (2000). Helping clients forgive: An empirical guide for resolving anger and restoring hope. American Psychological Association.

Erikson, E. H. (1968). Identity, youth and crisis. New York: Norton.

Eyre, L. and Eyre, R. (1987). Life balance. New York: Ballantine.

Freshwater, D. and Robertson, C., 2002. Emotions and needs (Buckingham) p. 26.

Freud S. (1923). The ego and the id. XIX (2nd ed.), Hogarth Press, republished 1955.

Friedman, M. (1996). Type 'A' behavior: Its diagnosis & treatment. New York: Plenum.

Frijda, N.H. (1986). The emotions. Cambridge: Cambridge University Press.

Gentry, W.D. et al. (1999). Habitual anger-coping styles: Effect on mean blood pressure and risk for essential hypertension, Psychosomatic Medicine 44.

Gilbert, F. &Daffern, M. (2011). Illuminating the relationship between personality disorder and violence: Contributions of the general aggression model. Psychology of Violence. Advance online publication, May 23 doi: 10.1037/a0024089.

Greenberg, L.S. (2002). Emotion-focused therapy: Coaching clients to work through their feelings. Washington, DC: American Psychological Association.

Greenberg, L.S. and Paivio, S.C. (1997). Working with emotions in psychotherapy. New York: The Guilford Press.

Greenberg, L.S., and Safran, J.D. (1987). Emotion in psychotherapy: Affect, cognition, and the process of change. New York: Guilford Press.

Gross, F. L. (1987). Introducing Erik Erikson: An invitation to his thinking. Lanham, MD: University Press of America.

Horwitz L. (2005). The capacity to forgive: Intrapsychic and developmental perspectives. J Am PsychoanalAssoc June 2005 vol. 53 no. 2 485-511.

Klein, M. (1975). Some theoretical conclusions regarding the emotional life of the infant. Envy and gratitude and other works 1946-1963. Hogarth Press and the Institute of Psycho-Analysis.

Klein, M. &Riviere, J. (1964). Love, guilt, and reparation. In Kohut, Heinz (1971). The analysis of the self: A systematic approach to the psychoanalytic treatment of narcissistic personality disorders. New York: International Universities Press.

Kristink, K., Wiafe A. (2010) Eight Steps to Overcoming Your Anger.

LeDoux, J. (1996). The emotional brain. New York: Touchstone.

McCullough, M. E. (2008). Beyond revenge. San Francisco: Jossey-Bass A Wiley Imprint 989 Market Street.

McMahon, G. (2008). No more anger. London: Karnac Books.

Mahler, S., Pine, M.M., and F. Bergman, A. (1973). The psychological birth of the human infant. New York: Basic Books.

Mahoney, M. (1993). Theoretical developments in the cognitive psychotherapies. Journal of Consulting and Clinical Psychology, 61, 187-193.

Meichenbaum, D. H. (1976). A cognitive-behavior modification approach. In M. Hersen& A. Bellack (Eds.), Behavioral assessment: A practical handbook. New York: Pergamon Press.

Menninger, W. (2007). Uncontained rage: A psychoanalytic perspective on violence. Bulletin of the Menninger Clinic, Vol. 71, No. 2.

Morrison, A. (1996). The culture of shame - The underside of narcissism. New York: Ballantine Books.

Neihoff, D. (1998). The biology of violence. New York: Free Press.

Novaco, R.W. (2005). Anger control: The development and evaluation of an experimental treatment. Lexington, Mass: D. C Heath, Lexington Books.

Paivio, S. C. (1999). Experiential conceptualization and treatment of anger. Journal of Clinical Psychology, Special Issue: Treating Anger in Psychotherapy, Volume 55, Issue 3, pages 311-324.

Potter-Efron, R.T. (2001). Stop the anger now. Oakland, CA: New Harbinger Pub.

Potter-Efron, R.T. (2004). Anger all the time. Raincoast Books.

Potter-Efron, R.T. (2007). Rage - A step-by-step guide to overcoming explosive anger. Raincoast Books.

Potter-Efron. R.T. (2005). Handbook for Anger Management. Hawthorne Taylor and Francis.

Seligman, M.E.P. (1994). What you can change & what you can't. New York: Alfred A. Knopf.

Selye, H. (1965). The stress of life. New York: McGraw-Hill.

Siegman, A.W. (1990). The angry voice: Its effects on experience of anger & cardiovascular reactivity. Psychosomatic Medicine 52.

Speakman, M. Resentment and the Three sources of Anger, May 2013

Sternberg, R. J. (Ed.) (2005). The psychology of hate. Washington, D.C.: American Psychological Association.

Tavris, C. (1989). Anger - The misunderstood emotion. New York: Simon & Schuster Inc.

Tomlinson, B. E. (1941). The psychoeducational clinic. New York, NY, US: MacMillan Co.

Weidner, J., Rice, R. and Knox, S. (2000). Familial resemblance for hostility. Psychosomatic Medicine 62:120-130.

Weisman, A. D. (1984). The coping capacity - On the nature of being mortal. New York: Human Sciences Press.

Winnicott, D. W. (1965). The family and individual development. London: Tavistock Publications.

Winnicott, D. W. (1973). The child, the family, and the outside world. Reading, Mass.: Addison- Wesley.

Worthington, E. (1998). Dimensions of forgiveness: Psychological research and theological perspectives. Philadelphia: Templeton Foundation Press.

Worthington, E. (2003). Forgiving and reconciling: Bridges to wholeness and hope. Downers Grove, IL: Intervarsity Press.

IF YOU NEED HELP....
We are HERE

If you or a loved one struggle with Anger, Addiction, Compulsions or Mood Disorders, and you are seeking help to manage the condition, you can register for our coaching program by logging onto www.Resolveinlove.com. You are also free to contact us by phone at 888.318.8027 or email us at info@resolveinlove.com

Our Coaching community has many people taking the same journey ready to talk and support you with whatever issues you may be facing. This community includes weekly webinars, forums, mobile apps, articles, videos, and many tools to assist and guide you through this challenge The million dollar question for all our participants during this challenge is " Will you Lose Control?" Join this life changing journey by accessing our community website at www.emotionalmillionaire.org/em-community.

If you wish to receive daily affirmations to keep you encouraged during your journey, you can text Iresolve to 76000 and you will start receiving life changing messages each morning by text to get you going strong.

EMOTIONAL
MILLIONAIRE SERIES
Resolving In-Love Consistently and Habitually

www.ingramcontent.com/pod-product-compliance
Lightning Source LLC
Chambersburg PA
CBHW081514040426

42447CB00013B/3219